"*An essential read for podcasters, salespeople, startup founders, and anyone who wants to lead deeper conversations with people they admire. Andrew Warner's book not only teaches you how to interview, it teaches you how to learn.*"

— Nir Eyal, bestselling author of
Hooked and *Indistractable*

"*Andrew Warner generously reveals how he mastered the craft of interviewing, giving readers a tactical roadmap to create winning conversations with people they admire.*"

— Espree Devora, host of *Women in Tech*,
Voted a Top 10 Podcast by *Harper's Bazaar*

"*This is a book about respect. Respecting others enough to interview them well. Respecting your audience enough to do the work. And respecting yourself enough to be clear about what you're doing and why.*"

— Seth Godin, founder of Akimbo (home of the
AltMBA) and author of 20 bestselling books

"*In the field of interviewing, Andrew is the archetypal example of 'so good they can't ignore you.' Read this book to steal his secrets!*"

— Chris Guillebeau, author of
The Money Tree and *The $100 Startup*

"*This book is not only a guide for interviewers like me, but is essential for anyone who wants to meet and learn from people a few steps ahead in life or business.*"

— Jordan Harbinger, host of *The Jordan Harbinger*
⋅ ⁿ Podcast

D1498502

Stop Asking Questions

Stop Asking Questions

HOW TO LEAD HIGH-IMPACT INTERVIEWS AND LEARN ANYTHING FROM ANYONE

Andrew Warner

The comprehensive guide to hosting better interviews for podcasters, salespeople, entrepreneurs, and more. Lessons from a veteran podcast host with 2,000+ episodes.

Published by Damn Gravity Media
damngravity.com
in partnership with Holloway
holloway.com

For rights and permissions, contact:
hello@damngravity.com

Print cover design by Dream Achievers
Interior design by Joshua Levy and Jennifer Durrant
Print engineering by Titus Wormer

Typesetting by Holloway in Tiempos Text and National 2
by Kris Sowersby of Klim Type Foundry

Ben Putano, Publisher · John Paul Hernandez, Social Media Manager ·
Joshua Levy, Publisher (Holloway) · Nathaniel Hemminger, Production
(Holloway) · Carolyn Turgeon, Editor (Holloway)

Print version 1.1.0
doc f7e764 · pipeline c70a6f · genbook 2fc993 · 2021-11-18

Want More Out of This Book?

We invite you to upgrade to the complete digital package, the Holloway Edition of *Stop Asking Questions*.

What's included:

- Lifetime access to the entire online book, including future updates and corrections
- Audio clips of the described interview techniques in action
- Video tutorial on Andrew Warner's podcasting process
- Access to 2,000+ Mixergy interviews ($400 value)
- Online interview course ($250 value, released Spring 2022)
- 270+ links and references

Read, watch, listen, and *master* the craft of interviewing.

As a purchaser of this print book or ebook, you can upgrade at a special price by visiting:

holloway.com/saqnow

TABLE OF CONTENTS

INTRODUCTION

To Olivia, who has embraced my curious spirit since our first date.

1 Acknowledgments

This book and the interviews it's based on couldn't have happened without the support, mentorship, and hard work of the people who helped me through it all.

Without the Damn Gravity Media team, this book wouldn't have been as good and hardly anyone would have known about it. I'm especially grateful to Ben Putano, the founder, who has talked with me practically every weekday since we started working together. Thank you for spending hours at your laptop telling people about my book and pushing me to stop being shy about promoting it. I don't know how you could be such a calm, encouraging coach with all the work you have on your plate. Thank you.

John Hernandez, thanks for turning the ideas in this book into content that spreads. My Twitter account never had as much action before you.

To the Holloway team—especially Joshua Levy and editor Carolyn Turgeon—thank you for helping me turn this book into something much more—an interactive digital resource for interviewers and conversationalists.

Thank you, Seth Godin and Tim Ferriss, for being some of my earliest guests. For years, every single one of my interview requests included a line about how you two did interviews with me. You helped me land great interviewees.

Paul Graham and Jessica Livingston, thank you for letting me promote my early interviews on Hacker News and introducing me to Y Combinator founders to interview. Your community created a solid foundation for me to build mine on.

Jason Fried, when I started charging for my interviews it felt like a world of criticism hit me online. Your supportive message kept me from backing down and helped me turn interviewing from a passion project to a business.

Jeremy Kareken, thank you for analyzing my interview transcripts with me in the hunt for the perfect questions and helping me realize that asking questions isn't the only way to get answers.

Noah Kagan, thanks for introducing me to your seemingly infinite number of friends. How do you know so many people?!

Neil Patel, when my site wasn't optimized and you got tired of telling me how to fix it, you took my username and password and fixed it yourself. Thanks for always being the person I could trust with my private information and jumping in to help so many times.

Arie Desormeaux, I once learned about a friend and interview guest who cried during their pre-interview with you. He thanked me for finding a producer who was so good at tapping into old memories. When I asked you why you didn't tell me about this, you said it happens too often to tell me every time. You have a gift for conversations. I'm lucky to have you at my side, shaping the stories we publish on *Mixergy*.

Andrea Schumann, you started out taking on small tasks at Mixergy and were always so good at your work. Over the years, you've done every job at the company. Thank you for keeping the company going and being someone I could count on.

Sachit Gupta, thanks for seeing our revenue and saying, "Andrew, you can do better." Then taking on the work of growing that revenue.

To the producers who've worked on *Mixergy*, you were responsible for preparing Silicon Valley's top founders to tell their stories and building an audience to hear them. Thank you, Giang Biscan, David Saint, AnneMarie Ward, Brian Benson, Tristan De Montebello, Joe Garcia, Rebecca Lay, Adrian Palma, Tam Pham, and Megan Johnson.

Jeremy Weisz, I used to get frustrated when you told me after each interview, "Yeah, but let's see how it could have been better," and "We need to talk every week." I thought I didn't have time. I'm glad you pushed me to make time.

Thank you, Michael and Marisela Khalili, for running Mixergy better than I ever could.

Bob Hiler, on our weekly calls you helped me understand that I needed to put a proper structure behind the loose collection of habits that formed *Mixergy*. The podcast couldn't have grown without you, and neither could I.

Rachel Kersten, you always had a better sense of the business side of content creation than I did. Thank you for professionalizing it.

Listeners who listened to my podcast over the years heard me mention several times that I was writing a book, but I could never sit down long enough to actually finish it. Then COVID-19 hit and Robbie Abed asked me to write a chapter for his book. He then encouraged me to keep writing and introduced me to people who could help. Thank you, Robbie.

Merry Sun, this book wouldn't have been finished if you hadn't gotten on calls with me every week to check on my progress, give me feedback, and guide me. Thank you for not quitting on me on all those times I said I needed to stop writing.

Ryan Holiday, I wanted support when I told you this book was too much work and I wanted to hire a ghost-writer. Thanks for giving me tough love instead. Writing it myself was the tougher, but better, approach.

Thank you, Taylor Jacobson and everyone at Focusmate. Whenever I needed to stay focused on writing, I'd start a session and instantly have a stranger to keep me going remotely via webcam on my phone.

To Chemda of the *Keith and the Girl* podcast, for showing me how powerful podcasts can be by sending me photos of fans with your logo tattooed on them.

To Mom and Dad. When my grade school teachers complained to you that I was a jack-in-the-box who couldn't sit still in class, instead of telling me I had to sit down, you asked the teachers if they'd allow me to have a desk in the back of their classes so my occasional need to stand up wouldn't disturb the other students. Thanks for always showing me that I don't have to accept the rules.

Thank you, River and Shepard, for being interested in the endless stories I tell at the dinner table about the amazing people I meet at work. And for always asking, "Can I do that?" Yes, you can do all of that. And more.

Finally, thank you, Olivia, my wife and soulmate, for always being patient when I use my interview skills to meet new people wherever we go. And for supporting me as I made one last attempt to write this book on that gorgeous dining room table you bought us. I love you.

2 Don't Miss Your Ace Opportunity

Billionaires turned to finance legend Alan "Ace" Greenberg for advice. He ran the Wall Street firm Bear Stearns at its prime. I was an unpaid college intern and wanted to learn from his experience. So I asked for a meeting and hoped he'd agree to the type of connection that could change my life. He said he wanted to help ambitious employees like me, so he set aside time for us to talk.

I walked in to see him, holding a notebook full of research I did based on obscure articles and conversations with people who followed his career. He sat at the end of a giant table he shared with dozens of his employees, most of whom seemed to be talking on two phones at once. It was loud, but his eyes and attention were only on me, eager to help. That's when it hit me. I didn't know how to access any of his wisdom.

I asked him about his start. He told me how he sat next to the firm's chairman and slowly took on more of the man's work until he was the firm's leader. I had already read that in an old *Forbes* article. So I asked what makes someone successful. He told me that instead of an MBA, he likes people with a PSD, which stood for "poor, smart, and a desire to be rich." I had read that in an old *BusinessWeek* article.

He was warm and attentive, but I couldn't figure out how to go deeper and learn anything new. Finally, he stood up and ended our mutual discomfort. Shaking my hand to indicate it was time for me to leave, he said, "A fella once told me, 'If you're doing what you enjoy, you never have to work a day in your life.' I hope that quote helps you."

I knew I'd missed a golden opportunity, but I wasn't sure what I'd done wrong. It was my one shot to tap into Ace Greenberg's wisdom, and all I got were facts I'd read before and some canned advice I could have found on my college bulletin board.

Today, we all have a world of opportunities to have conversations with people who could change our lives. Anyone with a computer or phone can record an interview, learn from people they admire, and share it with the world. Interview podcasts democratized access to these conversations. YouTube allows anyone with a camera to distribute their video interviews instantly. Blogging offers a place for text-based interviews. I've even seen one-minute interviews on TikTok gain hundreds of thousands of views. New online platforms are popping up constantly.

Offline opportunities are growing too. Conferences, meetups, and other events use interviews as an alternative to the traditional presentation.

Let's be real, though. Most of these interviews are simply insipid content thrown together by people who don't know how to tap into someone's greatness. I don't blame the interviewers. Nobody taught any of us this new craft.

Until the 1900s, publishing interviews was virtually unheard of. It was an ingredient in good journalism but hardly ever the finished product. Late-night TV talk show hosts were the ones who popularized the interview format. They needed an easy way for celebrities to shine without roping them into skits or other elaborate performances. From there, interview-based news shows became the work of serious journalists, who made their reputations by getting politicians and other newsmakers to reveal shocking information.

It was never my goal to create "gotcha" moments in interviews. I wanted to learn from people I admired—my heroes. I was desperate to improve.

Even though I graduated with a degree in finance, I didn't end up working in a bank or investment firm. I fell in love with entrepreneurship and started an online greeting card site that did over $30M in revenue. After selling it and taking a few years off, I came back to the startup life with an online invitation site. It completely bombed. It was so bad that even my wife refused to use it when she threw me a birthday party. I blew $300K on the business, but what really hurt was that I didn't know *why* I'd failed. I couldn't move forward with my business life until I knew how I could do better next time.

I became obsessed with interviewing after that second company failed. I sought out conversations with successful founders I admired to understand how to build a better business. I wasn't just hanging out with my guests. I was determined to use my interviews to become a better entrepreneur—a better me.

Unexpectedly, interviewing became my business. I started a podcast interviewing proven tech startup entrepreneurs like the founders of Airbnb, Dropbox, and Y Combinator. In each interview, I learned a bit more about how to run a company, including growing an audience, systemizing operations, and hiring. That grew into Mixergy,[1] a site for ambitious entrepreneurs.

Other entrepreneurs were equally eager to learn how to build a better company. As they showed up to listen to my episodes, advertisers bought ads to reach them. My interviews got so good that fans paid to listen to them and take my master classes.

---

1. https://mixergy.com/

Over the course of ten years, I interviewed more than two thousand people I admired. No one ever taught me how to interview, but I seized the opportunity behind every conversation by studying the hell out of the questions I asked and the responses I got.

In the years that followed, I spent $38,188 to have my interviews transcribed. Then I hired producers and coaches to go over my conversations to help find patterns in the responses. If a technique worked, I added it to a doc so I could keep reusing it. When something didn't work, I deconstructed it to understand how I should have done it better. The improved version went into the doc.

At some point, I shared my doc with my team so they could use the techniques to improve the conversations they had with guests when preparing them for my interviews. When other interviewers heard about it, they asked for copies. And when they started sharing it, I decided to organize it better, add more details, and turn it into the book you're reading.

I realize now what was missing when I talked with Ace. I wanted to learn, and he wanted to teach, but that desire is not enough. Interviewing is more than just asking questions. It takes skill to help someone teach what we want to understand—skills I've spent thousands of hours learning to master. The doc I created organized the skills I'd accumulated through interviewing. I'm sharing them with you so you can improve your podcast or in-person interviews, or simply have better conversations with people you care about.

This book is organized into four parts, following the order I've used when teaching new interviewers over the years. I noticed people first want quick, actionable techniques. So Part I is full of conversation tips you can master quickly and use for the rest of your life, in both interviews and daily conversations.

Once I give you the quick wins, you'll probably want to do the deeper, harder work of learning how to prepare for and structure an interview. So that's Part II. Then, when you have your skills nailed, you'll be eager to land your ideal interviewees. Part III focuses on how to identify good guests and convince them to sit for an interview. Finally, Part IV will give you the fundamental aspects of the business side of interviewing. If you can't make interviewing profitable, it'll be harder to make it sustainable.

As I mentioned, this format is based on how others I worked with preferred to learn. If you have different preferences, feel free to jump around. Just avoid limiting yourself to what you think you need. Conversations are unpredictable.

◇ CAUTION   One final piece of advice: Don't be rigid. You can't force each of these techniques into a conversation. Use them as guides, but don't be obsessed with using them perfectly. I don't. You're about to get to know and learn from your heroes. Enjoy it.

PART I: HIGH-IMPACT CONVERSATION TECHNIQUES

3 Simple Techniques for Better Conversations

In this first part, I'll fire you up with quick wins. These are conversation superpowers that you can master quickly. They'll get you past the toughest parts of your interviews, but they'll also work in non-interview conversations like dinners, parties, and meetings.

They're so fun and effective that they feel like party tricks. Using them is an easily mastered way of leveling up your interviews in the short term. In the next part, I'll cover how to make interviews meaningful and interesting.

20 TECHNIQUES
for
HIGH-IMPACT CONVERSATIONS

SETTING UP A CONVERSATION

"What's a Win for You?"	*The Promotion Stopper*	*Pre-ask the Shocking*
GET ON THE SAME PAGE	BLOCK AGGRESSIVE SELLING	STUN YOUR AUDIENCE WITH AUDACITY

LEADING HIGH-IMPACT CONVERSATIONS

Stop Asking Questions	*Share Your Why*	*Reciprocation*
DON'T SOUND NEEDY—LEAD THE CONVERSATION	HELP OTHERS GO DEEPER	MAKE OTHERS COMFORTABLE BY BEING OPEN ABOUT YOURSELF
Use Icon Stories	*Share a Higher Purpose*	*Home Run Questions*
RECRUIT THEIR HEROES TO HELP YOU	ENCOURAGE THEM TO JOIN YOUR MISSION	END ON A HIGH NOTE

CONVERSATIONAL TACTICS

Join the Resistance	*"Because?"*	*"Sorry to Interrupt …"*
GET GUARDED PEOPLE TO OPEN UP	SHORTEN LONG-WINDED RESPONSES	SMOOTHLY CUT OFF GUESTS WITHOUT OFFENCE
Stop Asking "Most" Questions	*Use Double-Barreled Questions*	*The Dramatic Lowball*
AVOID INTERVIEWERS' WORST QUESTIONS	HOW TO ASK QUESTIONS YOU SHOULDN'T ASK	GET THEM TO BLURT THE TRUTH

"A Time When You …"	*Put the Words in Someone Else's Mouth*
DRAW OUT INTERESTING STORIES	ASKING TOUGH QUESTIONS

DURING CONVERSATION

Look for Shoved Facts	*Avoid Train Crashes*	*The Talking Release*
DISCOVER TOPICS THEY CRAVE TO TALK ABOUT	HOW TO RECOVER FROM A NERVOUS MISTAKE	REMEMBER THE MAGIC OF LISTENING

An overview of techniques we'll cover in Part I.

Visit **holloway.com/saq-convos** for a more extensive online cheat sheet.

4　"What's a Win for You?"

Get on the Same Page

Timothy Sykes was at it again.

Looking at him through my webcam, I could see the winning smile of a man who expected to get the better of any conversation.

I asked him about his work ethic, and he managed to turn it into a pitch. "I have a DVD called Penny Stocking where I teach people ... And not surprisingly, my real-time stock trade alert service is fifty times more popular than this DVD that would actually teach them to do it on their own."

I asked him how he started blogging. "*Wall Street Warriors*," he said. "It's a hit TV show now in fourteen countries, so I was in that show, in five to six episodes of season one." Then he artfully mentioned his book, telling me, "People were emailing me what they wanted to know. So I wrote a book called *An American Hedge Fund*."

Honestly, I was in awe of how skilled he was at pushing his products, but I couldn't spend 60 minutes like that. I interviewed Tim because he quickly turned a blog into a $45K-per-month revenue machine, which he then used to fund a collection of finance software and marketplace sites. Mixergy had become both a passion and a content business, so I wanted to learn how he got people to his site and how he monetized his content.

My audience wanted to learn too. That's why they listened. Not to hear him plug his products.

After Tim's interview, I leaned back in my chair and tried to figure out how to stop situations like this. They happened often. And most interviewees weren't even as deft at self-promotion as Tim, leading to even more awkward interviews. Most were like jackhammers, hoping that determined repetition would help them break through. Heavy-handed promotion would ruin my podcast the way it ruined many other podcasts.

I wasn't mad. As an entrepreneur myself, I understood. When you run a company, you have big responsibilities. If you don't sell, you don't eat. And if you have a team, their families don't eat either.

That's when I realized something. They were pushing their goals out of desperation. To tell them "don't pitch" would be like saying "don't eat." What if I could assure them they'd get what they needed? If they knew their goals would be met, couldn't they chill out and enjoy being interviewed?

I tried something new while preparing for an interview. Before recording, I asked my guest, **"What's a win for you?"** That did it. Asking someone about their goals reassured them that I cared about their needs and that I'd work with them to reach those goals.

A typical example of this happened when I talked with Adam Jackson, who founded multiple companies, including MarketSquare, the local shopping site he sold to Intuit. When we connected, he had a serious look on his face and seemed to be distracted. I asked him, "What's a win for you?" He looked taken aback by the question. He smiled. Then he said, "You know, I feel like it already is a win because you asked that."

Adam told me he wanted to talk about how he disagreed with the way funding works in Silicon Valley. That was unexpected. He raised $23M for his latest startup,

Braintrust, the talent marketplace. I came into the conversation thinking he was a typical Valley fundraiser, but he wanted to argue against the system that I assumed he mastered. He also said he likes to get "outside the box a little bit," meaning he wanted a loosely structured conversation. Another blow to my plan, which was to take him through a hero's journey outline, a technique you'll learn about in the sections on interview structures.^{§25}

No problem. I quickly scribbled notes about what he said at the top of my interview doc. After I introduced him, I set him up to verbally punch the fundraising process and talk about the problems he had raising money. It was illuminating to see how much trouble he had because his business plan had a unique twist: he gave financial upside to participants of his marketplace. Once we talked about that, he was more than happy to give me what I was after—the chronological story of how he built and sold multiple companies.

If I hadn't asked about his needs, he might have gone along with my approach, but there would have been an underlying tension in the conversation that I couldn't have understood.

Most guests don't have a clear answer to "what's a win for you?" Sometimes their marketing team has recommended they do the interview. Sometimes they just accept the interview request because they like me. They don't have a goal or agenda. That's fine too. When I ask the question, even if they don't have a specific answer, they know I care about them and they trust that I have their interest in mind, even as I pursue my own interview goals.

Now I start most of my calls with some version of "what's a win for you?" Variations on that question include:

- What's your #1 goal for this interview?
- What would make your team happy to hear us talk about?
- Why did you agree to do this interview?
- How can I make this interview as useful for you as it will be for me and my listeners?

Try it. You'll see that if you show interest in your interviewee's goals, they'll help you hit your own goals.

5 Join the Resistance

Get Guarded People to Open Up

I wasn't being a jerk when I pushed Jason Fried to tell me about his failures. I acknowledged and admired how he bootstrapped Basecamp into a project management tool that was bringing in millions of dollars a year in profits.

Still, I wanted to hear about his failures. I learn a lot about growing a business by understanding how people overcome failures. But if I'm honest, I was also hoping to see that he was like me: a human being with failures I could relate to.

So I pushed. And pushed. And pushed. Finally, he looked right at his webcam—on a video call, the closest thing to looking someone in the eye—and told me that it's not helpful to even think about failures or look back.

Years later, when I hired Jeremy Kareken, an interview coach, I brought up this interview as an example of a big problem I have. In conversations, pushing harder for a goal often leads me further away from the goal.

"Ah," he said. "Join the resistance, Andrew."

He explained that he learned this technique from his therapist, who encountered similar types of resistance. In couple's therapy, when she pushed male patients to be open—to use their time as an opportunity to bring up problems and work through them—the men would resist with comments like, "I don't have any problems."

The therapist used to push back. She tried explaining that everyone has problems, that the reason a patient was in her office week after week was that he obviously had challenges to work through. None of it worked.

Finally, instead of pushing back against a patient's resistance, she decided to **join the resistance**. "It seems like everything is going well," she'd say. "It's nice for me to get to talk to someone who has an easy life, who has it good."

That did it. "Easy?" her patient would ask in shock. "You don't know how hard things really are. Just this week ..." And suddenly, the conversation was productive.

To see how powerful this technique is in interviews, let me tell you about the next interview I did with Jason *after* I'd learned it.

We talked about how he had a massive hit with HEY, his new email service and software. Within 30 days, HEY had 170K people on its waitlist and generated $5M in revenue. His approach was to start from scratch, ignoring how email had worked since its inception. He simply asked himself and his team what they wanted from email. That's how they decided to create a gatekeeper section, which doesn't allow anyone to reach users' inboxes without prior permission.

After hearing about what went well, I brought out my new technique. "Everything seems to work for you," I said, referring to the products he'd launched over the years. "Great for you."

This got Jason's attention. He started listing software he'd created that didn't go nearly as well as his big successes. Campfire, for example, was a business chat software, like Slack. Slack ended up becoming a multibillion-dollar, publicly traded company. Campfire was sunsetted. His list went on.

Still, these setbacks didn't damage his company because he didn't bet the business on them. Business books often recommend that founders become like the general who storms the beach and burns his soldiers' boats behind him. With no option but to win, the soldiers are said to be forced into invincibility. Entrepreneurs are also told to take big risks that keep them from backing out.

What I learned from Jason was that it's sometimes preferable to take smaller risks. It's OK to close a business, even if others would consider it a massive failure. What Jason learned from creating Campfire informed the chat feature in Basecamp, his massively successful project management software.

Next time you're trying to get someone to be vulnerable and tell you about their challenges, don't push back against their resistance if they put up roadblocks. Accept it. And even congratulate them for it. They say, "I never failed." You say, "It's amazing to talk to someone who always got everything right." They say, "I'm not a worrier." You say, "I don't usually get to talk to people who are 100% confident."

Did I trick Jason into sharing his failures? Am I telling you to use "join the resistance" to make people reveal their secrets to you?

I've interviewed Jason seven times in the past decade. He keeps returning even though he knows I'm going to push him to be open. He returns because he trusts me.

I have a recording of the first time I used the "join the resistance" technique. If you watch carefully, you'll see him doing something that others have done when I encouraged them to be open. He peeks up at his computer screen to see my face. He's checking me out to see if he should trust me, if I'm being sincere, if it's safe to talk.

◇ CAUTION If you have bad intentions, you might trick someone once, but they'll resent you for it. And they won't want to talk to you again. If your motives are grounded in a need to get real understanding, they'll appreciate that you helped them open up.

6 Look for Shoved Facts

Discover Topics They Crave

A few years ago, I had several guests over for dinner.

We all sat around my living room, waiting for the last guest to arrive.

Finally, as he came in, he said, "Sorry I'm late, everybody. When you go through a divorce, everything takes longer, like finding your daughter's sweater. Plus, traffic is getting rough in this city."

One of the other guests said, "I know what you mean about traffic. As the tech industry grows, people keep piling into San Francisco and causing congestion everywhere."

Another said, "Well, you're here now. Sit down and relax."

We sat down to dinner and talked about superficial things, like how San Francisco is changing and why it never seems to be sunny here.

What a missed opportunity.

Most people fail to recognize the most meaningful conversation topics. Our friend shared something I call a "shoved fact." He didn't need to mention his divorce. He could have simply said "traffic is awful in this city," and everyone would have related and moved on. But he intentionally pushed his divorce into the conversation. He was dying to talk about it because it was a big issue for him. He brought it up, and none of us acknowledged it.

The **shoved fact** is very similar to the psychoanalysis term "Freudian slip," which says a slip of the tongue may represent an unconscious wish or internal train of thought. As conversationalists, we often ignore the teeny slips of the tongue because they're mostly meaningless. The average person slips on up to 22 words per day.[2] But when someone pushes a big topic out of context, we need to be aware that they might be expressing a yearning to talk about it—especially during an interview.

I ask *Mixergy*'s producers to look for shoved facts as part of the pre-interview process. So when producer Arie Desormeaux pre-interviewed Chris Martinez, founder of DUDE, the website and design agency, he said that he played soccer and mentioned that he got into it to escape his abusive childhood. Arie noted down the shoved fact.

On the day of the interview, I asked Chris about it, and he opened up about being beaten as a child. He cried while telling me about the time his mom pulled over their car and didn't stop hitting him until she noticed people watching. The story was painful to hear, and I'm sure even more so to tell, but it helped me understand his super-power. As an entrepreneur, Chris wasn't held back by embarrassment the way others might be.

He then told me a great story to illustrate the point: After Chris moved his digital agency to Tijuana, Mexico, he noticed that some clients were hesitant to work with him because of Tijuana's reputation. They couldn't stop thinking of Tijuana as the place Americans go to drink tequila, let go of rules, and have a raucous time.

Instead of trying to hide his home base from clients, Chris talked it up with pride. It became part of his marketing. He wore a Mexican wrestling costume at trade shows, which got attention at the buttoned-up events. When try-

2. Pincott, Jena E. "Slips of the Tongue."[3] *Psychology Today*, 2012.

3. https://www.psychologytoday.com/intl/articles/201203/ slips-the-tongue

ing to close a sale, he explained that his agency could charge less because of where it was located. After signing each client, he pulled out a bottle of tequila to celebrate.

Addressing his shoved fact helped me understand him better. It helped me understand his superpower. We're now a little closer because of it.

Look for those shoved facts, and don't be afraid to dive into them.

7 Reciprocation

Get Guests Comfortable with Transparency

After I sold my greeting card company, I moved to Santa Monica and took a few years off work to focus on personal development.

One of the best things I did was go to weekly Toastmasters[4] meetings to become a better speaker. I was still new there when one of the members invited us all to her house for drinks.

For the first hour, the conversation was stilted, limited to whether our cars could make it to the top of Bear Mountain without snow chains. Elena, one of the other guests, said: "I don't know if it could make it up a mountain, but I know it could go across the country. After my sister committed suicide, I put all my things in the backseat and drove till I got to California. It didn't give me any trouble on the way over. I've had it for seven years, and it's always held up."

Someone asked what type of car it was. By then I already knew how to spot a shoved fact, and how it's a signal that someone is eager to talk about a topic. So after she answered that she had a Ford Bronco, I asked a more meaningful follow-up.

"Do you feel comfortable saying more about your sister?" I asked. (In the section on double-barreled questions,[§18] you'll understand why I phrased my question this way.)

---

4. https://www.toastmasters.org/

She paused for a moment, then said, "She was battling depression for years, but my family didn't talk about it much. We thought it was something she'd just get through as she got older."

Someone else said, "My aunt went through that too. Back then it was an embarrassing thing to talk about. We thought people would blame us for causing it, or that her depression was contagious and would somehow rub off on them."

As Elena told us about her family, I asked a few more questions, and she kept opening up. She unburdened herself. The big secret she kept hidden didn't need to be a secret. It felt good to be accepted and to see she wasn't alone.

Then, as she wound down, she said something that hurt me. She leaned back into the sofa, crossed her legs, and said, "Andrew's always pumping us for personal information." I looked at her and saw resentment in her eyes.

I couldn't understand it. I knew she felt relief from talking. At times she cut me off and cut others off, just so she could keep telling us about her family. Why the hostility?

As I drove home that night, I couldn't stop thinking about Elena. I realized that as my conversation skills improved, some people felt relief and closeness by talking to me. But I also realized that some people said the same thing Elena did. They felt I was pumping them for information, even though I was tapping into what they were dying to talk about.

Mulling it over, I realized my mistake. I never shared anything revealing about myself. My conversation techniques worked so well that people opened up, often more than they ever had before. Yes, they felt relief and acceptance, but they also felt vulnerable. And, more painfully, they felt *alone* in their vulnerability.

So I started talking more about myself. At first, I tried keeping things balanced. I talked as much about myself as my conversation partners talked about themselves. Quickly, I discovered that most people don't want to listen. They prefer to talk.

What I've learned is to include a revealing sentence or two about myself every once in a while, then go back to giving others a chance to talk. That **reciprocation** is the right balance.

Once I figured that out, I asked Elena if she wanted to take a walk to the Coffee Bean & Tea Leaf for a drink after a Toastmasters session. When we sat down, I said, "I was curious about your sister because my brother dealt with depression in high school. I always wondered what I would do if I had kids who went through it. That's why I asked you about it the other night."

She started telling me about how she's been in therapy and what her family wished they'd done. We talked for two hours. Well, she did most of the talking. I was incredibly curious and loved listening. Every once in a while, I interjected with something personal about myself. When she finished her second cup of tea and was ready to go home, she said, "I like talking with you, Andrew. I feel like you're the only one who really understands me."

I reciprocate in interviews too. Robert LoCascio, founder of LivePerson, the $3B customer service software company, told me about the failure of his previous company. He lost almost everything he had, and he told me about how miserable he was, which finally led him to get a therapist. If you listen to that interview, you'll hear me share stories about my background, and how I was ashamed as a boy when my family's landline was shut off because we couldn't pay the bill. My little confessions made me feel relieved, but they also created an atmosphere where Robert could open up about his problems.

When Pablo Fuentes, founder of Proven, the small business hiring company, told me about failing nine times, I told him that one of my most painful worries is that if my business fails, I won't be able to get a job.

I add a line or two about myself when I ask guests to talk openly about themselves. I don't do it to take attention off them. I do it to make them feel safe enough to talk openly.

Other good podcasters do it too. Dax Shepard is an actor, director, and host of the hit podcast, *Armchair Expert*—the most downloaded new show on Apple Podcast in 2018. Shepard says people listen to his show because of the vulnerability of his guests. "I am so often trying to enact vulnerability," he said as a guest on *The Tim Ferriss Show*, "which requires me to go first. It's almost like an [Alcoholics Anonymous] meeting where it's like, I share first, and then maybe you're compelled to share back."

As you get good at using these conversation techniques, you'll get a deeper understanding of other people's lives. Make sure to share your life with them too.

When you share, be prepared to suddenly feel vulnerable and exposed. I did. One day on a coaching call with Jeremy Kareken, I announced that I was sick of how much of a sissy I was being. For minutes, he didn't respond. He kept reading the interview transcripts we were working on. Then he finally asked, "What do you mean?"

"I notice that bloggers, Instagrammers, podcasters, and others use their reach to show how amazing they are. They only show their strengths. Meanwhile, I can't stop bringing up my weaknesses in my interviews."

"For example?" he asked.

"Well, just look at the transcript you're going through right now. Within ten minutes I told my interviewee about one of my flaws. She responded by telling me how amazing she is. So now anyone listening will think of me as weak and her as successful."

No response. Jeremy kept his head in my transcript. Did he even care? He produced national television. Was helping a flawed interviewer like me so beneath him that my issues weren't even worth acknowledging?

I waited.

Then Jeremy said, "Scroll to page 15 of the transcript. That's where she tells you how her parents were incredibly hard on her and she felt like a failure as a child. Then she tells you how that led her to work harder, to prove herself to her parents. To fight back against what people thought of her."

I read the passage from the transcript. "Andrew, you shared," he continued. "You got vulnerable. You can't expect her to reciprocate instantly. This isn't a transaction where you trade your story for hers. You're setting the atmosphere, giving her space to share too. And she did. I've read dozens of your transcripts. I can't think of a single time that didn't happen ... eventually. But you need to be patient and trust." He was right.

"And you know what?" Jeremy said. "Sometimes the people you're talking with won't open up on the first conversation. It might take them years. Others won't open up at all. You need to be fine with that."

Today I am fine with that, but only because I saw how often it's true. If you want people to be open with you, you need to be willing to share first, and to do it without an expectation for immediate reciprocation. Give it time. The depth of your conversations will be worth it.

8 The Promotion Stopper

Block Aggressive Selling

After I started writing this book, I offered one-on-one coaching sessions with new interviewers to ensure I was addressing their real needs. Over and over, I saw that one of their biggest challenges was curbing excessive promotion. In the "What's a Win for You?" section,[§4] I addressed how to show a guest you understand their need for promotion. But when is the right time to finally help them promote?

In most cases, the answer is when you're interested in what they're promoting and when you think your audience would be curious about it. So if you're interviewing an author of a new book you enjoy, absolutely start by asking about it.

But if the promotion has nothing to do with why you're talking to them, wait until the end, when you and your audience are emotionally connected to the guest. That's how it's been done on television for years. When I was a kid, if Robert De Niro was doing a late-night interview, it wasn't because he enjoyed wincing through questions about his childhood. He had a new movie to promote. The deal was he'd give the interviewer a little peek into his life so fans like me could get to know one of our favorite actors. In return, the host's job was to help De Niro promote his latest movie.

I found that it's best to clarify the agenda with guests before we start recording by using a **promotion stopper**. I get their buy-in by phrasing it as a question, like, "Of course I'll mention your new project in my intro, but since my audience isn't emotionally connected to it yet, do you mind if we build your credibility first by talking about the big company you sold?"

They almost always agree. Occasionally someone will push back and say what they did before is boring and they want to talk about what they plan to do. When that happens, I remind them that my site's mission is to talk about how big achievers built their companies. The audience would feel cheated if I promised that and gave them something else.

If they still insist on promoting their new thing, I'm comfortable forfeiting the interview, but it's never come to that. People understand. Each show has its own approach, and if they want to be on, they need to work with it. No guest would go on Comedy Central's *The Daily Show* and complain that Trevor Noah cracked too many jokes.

Sometimes, a guest might get excited about their new project and start talking about it in the middle of me asking questions about their previous startup. I quickly say, "We'll get to that, but first let's finish talking about how you got here."

When guests see me keep control of the conversation and promise to meet their needs, they share more and promote less. It's a win-win.

9 Share Your Why

Help Guests Go Deeper

Have you ever met someone who seems so perfect that they feel fake? I was starting to feel that way in my interview with Taro Fukuyama. So I wanted him to tell me about something that didn't go well.

I asked if Fond, the employee reward company he launched (previously called AnyPerk), had hit its first million dollars.

"More than that," he shot back.

Well, how about the customers? He started listing blue chip brands that signed up with him: Virgin America, Salesforce, Cushman & Wakefield. Then he explained that they were just the tip of the iceberg.

Isn't competition heavy? "Actually, we don't have that many competitors right now."

I can't blame him for talking up his company. As the founder, his job was to promote his company's success on my podcast. Plus, he deserved to be proud. A few years before, he was sleeping outside a Taco Bell, listening to my interviews, planning to be as successful as the entrepreneurs I talked with.

Still, the reason people listen to my interviews is to learn from my guests. They want to see how successful founders get past the kinds of obstacles they're likely to face.

How could I get him to talk about a failure? A setback that might have a valuable lesson for my listeners?

I ended up using a technique that's always worked for me: I told him what I wanted and *why* I wanted it. I call this **"share your why."**

"Tell me about a time you were depressed," I said. "Let me see that you're human, not just a guy who's a beaming Tony Robbins Jr."

"Oh." His attitude changed. "This is my first company. I didn't know how to run a company. I didn't know how to manage people." The conversation went in a new direction.

He explained that when investors pressured him to grow faster, he started "managing people by anger." He would say, "Hey, you've got to do this. You have to stay until X time because I'm staying until 11 p.m. every day."

That's not the type of attitude the founder of an employee engagement company would usually fess up to. But every leader can relate to his pressure. And it was valuable to learn how he went about solving his problem by talking to his employees one-on-one, taking responsibility for creating a happy and productive culture.

I didn't realize how often I used this technique until I talked with Ashwin Vishwanathan, a banker and regular *Mixergy* listener from Singapore. I met up with Ashwin when I recorded a few interviews in his home country. Unprompted, he said he heard me use the "share your why" technique so often that he started using it at his work. Just like I do in my interviews, I asked him for specifics. He hit me with a story that proves this technique works even outside of interviews.

He told me that when he decided to quit banking, his boss's boss called him in for a meeting. The executive, a dour man who was always stressed, ripped into Ashwin. "What are you doing? I heard you're quitting."

Ashwin gave a prepared answer and was met with a forceful stare. Then Ashwin looked at the executive and said, "What's your motivation?" That crossed a line. Too personal for a Singaporean banker. So Ashwin looked into his eyes and slowly said, "I'm asking because I've always wanted to be an entrepreneur. If I don't do it now, I'm worried I might never do it. I'm not sure how to find the motivation to give that dream up."

His boss paused, looked at him, and then started speaking with more empathy. He explained that he, too, once wanted to start a company. When he was ready to take the risk and quit his job, the bank gave him a raise. He stayed. Then he landed a promotion. Then another raise. The upward path was good, but it also locked his family into a lifestyle he couldn't give up. Now, with kids in expensive American schools, there was no way he could leave.

The executive spent 45 minutes reminiscing about his life and decisions with Ashwin. Then he ended by telling Ashwin that if he wanted to return to banking after entrepreneurship, there would be a home for him at his company.

Share your why. Give people a heartfelt reason to help you.

10　"Because?"

Shorten a Long-Winded Style

Even if you listened to each of my 2,000-plus interviews, you would probably miss my best question. That's because it's my shortest question. Ironically, it's also a question I stole from Charlie Rose.

Rose's iconic interview show lasted for a quarter century on PBS. But critics initially hated it because he asked questions that were longer than his guests' answers. It became so bad that Rose's long-windedness was parodied[5] on *Saturday Night Live*. In the skit, Rose (played by Jeff Richards) interviewed Donald Rumsfeld (Darrell Hammond) and droned on for so long that Rumsfeld erupted, "I think you just spent ten minutes asking me a question, but I have no idea what it is!" Finally, Rumsfeld walked off as Rose continued to struggle to explain what he's trying to ask.

I totally relate to Rose. There's so much I'm trying to cram into each question. I want people to go deeper and also know that I'm giving them a safe space to do it. I want to understand their motivation and tell them why I care. Sometimes I just get lost in my own sentences and can't find a way out.

But Rose kept improving. By the time I started interviewing, he was so smooth that everyone from Bruce Springsteen to Bill Gates appeared on his show. Business leaders paid him more than $50K to come to their corpo-

---

5. https://www.nbc.com/saturday-night-live/video/
　 charlie-rose-donald-rumsfeld/2869240

rate events and interview them onstage. They weren't paying for Charlie Rose per se, but for his ability to help them express themselves better than they could on their own.

As I studied his style, I noticed that he repeatedly asked one simple question: "Because?"

Before I explain why this question works, I have to show you an example of how I used that question in an interview I did with John Doherty, founder of Credo, a platform for hiring marketers.

> **Andrew:** *Your company was called HireGun?*
>
> **John:** *Yup. Yup. So we rebranded. Well, yeah, so this is—*
>
> **Andrew (interrupting):** *Because?*
>
> **John:** *We rebranded on January 16 because we launched on Product Hunt, and two weeks later, we landed in Virginia, where I'm from, for Thanksgiving. And I pulled my email, and I ha[d] a cease and desist letter in my email.*
>
> *It's like 6:00 p.m. on Thanksgiving Eve, and I had a cease and desist letter basically saying, "You're infringing on our copyright. You need to give us your website, everything, now!"*

John went on to tell the story of how he pushed back on the attacking company and saved his business.

The beauty of the one-word question **"because?"** is that it acknowledges that I heard what was said before and shows that I care about it so much that I want to understand the reason behind it.

It's elegantly simple. It's so short that I can slip it into an interviewee's long-winded monologue virtually unnoticed. They don't even realize I'm redirecting them towards a deeper discussion. If you think about the times you've used the word "because," you'll see that you often use it to transition from *what* you did to *why* you did it. For example, "I started interviewing *because* I wanted to learn how to build a successful company."

And that's my goal in every conversation: To go deeper, to understand why someone did what they did. To understand who they are. No other word in the English language spurs such a depth of understanding as "because."

11 The Dramatic Lowball

Get Them to Blurt the Truth

Over the years, I've been known to host events called Scotch Night at my office, where I invite a few *Mixergy* listeners to join me for a drink and conversation. I remember one particular evening well. Sitting on tall chairs around a long table, few paid attention to the variety of Scotch bottles I put out. It was all about the conversation. Each founder was eager to hear what was working at other companies, so the group was boisterous.

After an hour, a founder that the group called "College" (because he was still in school and not old enough to drink) asked, "Andrew, do you ever have a guest who won't say anything about their financials? How do you get them to be so open?" Everyone quieted down. As information hunters, it was something they also wanted to learn.

"Yeah," I said. "A few days ago, Shradha Agarwal, founder of ContextMedia, which does health videos for waiting rooms, wouldn't tell me anything about her revenue. I wasn't trying to pry—I just needed a sense of how big her company was so the audience could understand what we were talking about. She wouldn't give me anything."

"What'd you do?" he asked.

"I threw out a number that was absurdly low for her. I asked, 'Are you doing at least a million dollars in sales?' Instantly I felt her aggravation. She shot back, 'We're doing 20 or 30 times that!' That gave me my answer."

It worked because I lowballed her dramatically. I gave her a number that was almost an insult to the years of work and the amount of pride she had. Instinctively, she felt the need to correct the record.

College smiled when I explained that. He learned something he could use for getting partners for his side hustle. Then we moved on to random Scotch Night conversation, like my enjoyment of running.

"Are you still running?" College asked me.

"Yeah, I run a bit," I said modestly and tried to change the subject.

"Did you ever think about building up to a five-mile race?" he asked.

"Five miles? I do more than that when I run to this office every morning. I ran more marathons than I can count."

College didn't say anything, but I could see he was holding back a smile. Eventually, everyone else at the table started laughing.

It took me a moment. Then I realized what happened. College used a dramatic lowball on me. I laughed too.

But secretly, I was happy to share. Running is my passion. I'm proud of how far I can run, but I feel awkward talking about it because it feels like I'm boasting. So if you ask me about my running, even though I want to tell you about it, I'll hold back. The dramatic lowball gave me the push I needed. It made it OK for me to talk about something that I would otherwise hold inside.

As an interviewer, I noticed that people are taught from an early age not to brag, so they resist talking about their achievements. Our job as interviewers is to encourage them to do it. The **dramatic lowball** does that.

In fact, the dramatic lowball is so effective that I try not to use it in interviews. I don't edit my interviews, and I don't want to trick anyone into publicly releasing something they're not ready to share. So I reserve the technique for the conversations I have before interviews start.

You can hear how I used it with the heavily bearded Chris Stoikos, founder of Dollar Beard Club (since renamed The Beard Club), a men's grooming supplies company. During the pre-interview, I asked Chris if he was doing $1M in revenue. "No," he shot back.

He was doing nearly $1.5M every month.

I asked him what payment processor he used.

"Stripe."

"Can you do a screen share of Stripe to show me?" I asked.

So Chris logged in and showed me. He shared multiple dashboards, as if to prove how wrong my revenue guess was.

Afterward I was worried Chris regretted telling me. He said he didn't. He even gave me permission to publish both his revenue and the whole conversation we had before the interview. He was comfortable being open if it meant having more bearded men discover his grooming supplies.

◇ CAUTION Use the dramatic lowball technique with care. It can lead to such quick results that it can startle the person you're speaking with. Remember, our goal is to help people be open so we can learn from them.

12 Share a Higher Purpose

Encourage Them to Join Your Mission

When Gregg Spiridellis sat down for an interview with me, I had a sense he wasn't sure why he even agreed to do it. His production company, JibJab, was cranking out viral video after viral video. He'd even been featured on *The Today Show*. I wouldn't blame him for feeling odd about sitting in front of a webcam with someone he had never met as a favor to a friend whom I had interviewed a few days before.

"It's a challenging day," he told me when I asked how he was doing. How could I get his best effort when there was so much pulling at his attention?

Gregg was running one of the hottest content brands in the country. *ABC News* named him and his co-founder[6] People of the Year because their video, "This Land," went viral with a message of unity at a politically divisive time. Meanwhile, my podcast hadn't yet broken the 100-download barrier.

When I doubt myself, I remind myself of my mission. I want to get the true stories of how founders built their companies. I sensed that telling Gregg my vision in a way that showed him the benefit of participating would get him engaged.

Before we started recording, I looked into my webcam—the closest I could get to looking him in the eyes. I said, "Gregg, I want to record an interview so good that decades from now when your great-great-grandkids won-

---

6. https://abcnews.go.com/WNT/PersonOfWeek/story?id=369362

der how you built your business, they'll come listen to what we record today."

With that one sentence, I got his attention. When the interview began, he sat up in his chair and started telling me some private, never-before-told stories. Turns out that when he was on *The Today Show*, his company was struggling financially. So the night before, he and his brother came up with a quick way to make some money. They mocked up a DVD box that looked like it had their video on it. Then they created an online store.

When *The Today Show* cameras were on them, they held up the fake DVD box and said their video was for sale for $9.99 on their site. "We had no idea how we were going to fulfill those DVDs," he told me. But their site said it would take four to six weeks for shipping, so they knew they'd have time to figure it out. As a result, the first day the DVDs went on sale, they raised almost $100K in much-needed revenue.

As Gregg talked, I could see the smile on his face and the enthusiasm of someone who worked hard and finally had a chance to look back in awe of what he accomplished. When we were done, he told me that if he knew how important this interview was, he would have made an effort to look good on camera instead of just throwing on a baseball cap.

A few months after I published, he asked for a downloadable copy of his interview so his family could have it. I could tell he had bought into my mission. And it showed in the final interview. He hadn't just given me quick, superficial answers as a way of living up to a commitment.

Sharing my higher purpose has also helped me land interviews. One of the toughest pitches to potential guests was my Fail Series. Our producer, Tristan de Montebello, wrote a blog post on Mixergy asking entrepreneurs to spend an hour telling me how their companies failed. Not exactly an easy sell. Think about what they're risking. These founders will start future companies. They need investors and job candidates and co-founders to believe enough in their abilities to stake their careers and money on their venture.

Tristan explained how the interview series would help listeners avoid potentially fatal mistakes in their businesses. As tough as it would be for a founder to talk about their own failures, it would be a gift to other entrepreneurs like them. It would lead to stronger startups.

As a result of sharing our higher purpose, we ended up with more than a week's worth of interviews in this series. It created a ripple effect in the Mixergy community. When interviewees in the series talked about their mistakes, they did it with a spirit of support for other entrepreneurs. Listeners picked up on it and started spreading the word that Mixergy was a place to talk openly and safely about failures to help other entrepreneurs.

I can still feel the impact of that series to this day. Years later, Nikki Durkin of 99dresses, a platform for women to trade clothes, felt comfortable enough on my show to tear up and talk about losing her co-founders. Marcus Weller, the founder of Skully (the helmet with a built-in display), felt he could talk safely about being accused (and later cleared) of spending company money on strippers and sports cars.

Sharing your higher purpose helps beyond interviewing. When my wife and I moved to Washington, DC, we argued about how much I ran. I understood how she felt. We were both working long hours, and she wanted to see more of me. But DC was the first city I had lived in with parks everywhere. I wanted to run and experience all of them. So we argued.

I finally used what I learned in my interviews. I said, "Olivia, we both believe in pushing ourselves physically. I think I might be able to do my first solo 26.2-mile run, but I'm still at only 14 miles. Would you help me?"

That was a dramatic difference from my previous approach of saying, "You know how much I love running. I need time to do it. I can't give that part of myself up."

She bought into the goal of pushing myself to do a bigger run than I had ever done before. She even found ways to support it, like meeting me at the office after work so we could both run home together. On the weekends, if she had an appointment far from home, I'd drive there with her. She'd drive home alone and wish me well as I attempted to run home. Once, she dropped me off at the top of Rock Creek Park and then went to run errands. I had no choice but to run home, which was over 30 miles. We're both proud of that accomplishment.

In business, interviewing, and life, we often find ourselves needing to persuade and motivate other people. **Share a higher purpose** to get others on board with your goals. Give them a mission they can buy into and support.

13 Stop Asking Questions

Don't Sound Needy

Most people think an interviewer's job is to ask questions. I can tell you from experience that it's not.

I learned this at a hilltop house in Los Angeles overlooking the ocean. While my friend Steve and I had a beer by his pool, I asked him what he did to earn such a gorgeous place.

"We've known each other a long time because our wives are friends," I said. "But I never asked you about your business. What do you do, Steve?"

He said he made apps. I saw a quick smile come across his face, so I followed up with, "How'd you get started?"

That made him beam. He told me how he started creating apps for BlackBerry. He did it before Apple announced the iPhone, before the word "app" was known by the average person, and before the hottest hotshots in Silicon Valley had apps on their product roadmaps.

I was fascinated, so I asked him more questions. How did he know apps would be big? How did he make the transition to iPhone apps? How did he get his first customers?

As we chatted more about his company, his enthusiasm and pride grew. But when I got up to get another beer, he asked me to grab him one. Then he asked me if I needed help getting started in business. That's when I noticed the tone of our conversation was changing. We had started out as peers, but my incessant line of questioning made me sound like a student. Or worse, a needy intern. And he was treating me that way.

The same problem started creeping into my interviews. After a few questions in a row, I started to sound clueless.

"How did you get started?"

"How did you grow your company?"

"How could I do that?"

All curious people will encounter this problem. Asking questions makes you seem needy. And if you're needy, people don't respect you, which reduces the quality of their answers.

A couple of years into my interviewing career, I started to get a chip on my shoulder about being minimized by guests. I'm ashamed of some of the ways I reacted to it. My worst moment was waiting for Rod Drury, the founder of accounting software Xero. He was late, and I had a live audience watching me wait. I was embarrassed and aggrieved. So I started mocking him on camera for not caring. When he did show up a few minutes late and was incredibly nice, I felt like a jerk. I still feel guilty every time I see a Xero ad or hear a friend talk about how amazing his software is.

One of the ways I responded to that period of frustration was by taking charge of the conversation from the start. If the guest was in a loud room, I told them to move. I didn't ask. I said, "You need to find a quiet place to record, or the audience won't be able to hear your story." If they didn't have a strong internet connection, I told them to find a way to fix it, or we'd need to reschedule for a day when it would be better.

Guests appreciated that kind of leadership, so I brought the attitude into my interview. I rephrased my questions as directives. Instead of asking, "How did you get your first customer?" I said, "Tell me how you got your first customer."

At times it felt rude. Was I being bossy instead of kind? Did they think I was too demanding? Too pushy?

Not at all. In fact, switching about half my questions to statements changed how people saw me. They stopped treating me like a needy kid and saw me as a leader who would guide them through their interview. I no longer felt ashamed or resentful of perceived slights. It felt good to guide them toward telling the best possible stories.

Interviewees appreciated this direct approach. Being interviewed requires a lot of trust. Guests want a host who will keep them sounding interesting, helpful, and bring out stories they'd never think of on their own. That kind of guidance doesn't come from a needy intern. It comes from a leader. Real leaders use clear statements and make thoughtful requests.

If you were going hiking with a guide, you wouldn't want her to keep asking, "Do you want to go left or right?" She's the one with experience. It's her job to know what's down each path and to understand your interests well enough to pick for you. That's what your interviewees need from you. Guide them.

So **stop asking questions**. Start leading your guests through better conversations.

14 Put the Words in Someone Else's Mouth

Asking Tough Questions

I grew up in New York City, so I prefer to be blunt and ask for what I want. But as an interviewer, if I don't take some of the sting out of my questions, my guest could become defensive, stop paying attention, and maybe even walk off.

A good example of this comes from a BBC interview[7] with conservative commentator Ben Shapiro. The video went viral because he stormed out before it was over. I had the interview transcribed so I could study it and understand what the interviewer said to elicit that response.

Right from the start, the interviewer asked tough questions. "Haven't the conservatives run out of ideas in America?" he asked. Then he hit Shapiro with an observation that new ideas were really coming from the Left, instead of Shapiro's conservatives. Then he got under his skin by asking, "Why is it that a bill banning abortions after a woman has been pregnant for six weeks, is not a return to the Dark Ages?"

These are all legitimate questions for a conservative thinker, but reading how question after question unfolded, I understood why the barrage might make Shapiro feel personally attacked.

In response, Shapiro accused the interviewer of bias. "Why can't you just say you're on the left?" And he argued against almost every question he was asked. "Would you

---

7. https://www.youtube.com/watch?v=6VixqvOcK8E

ask the same question to a pro-choice advocate?" And eventually, he walked off.

In reality, the interviewer, Andrew Neil, chaired an organization that owned *The Spectator,* a right-wing magazine. So their politics weren't in opposition, but the tone of the questions felt combative.

If dramatic frustration like this is what you want from your guest, by all means, be blunt. Don't take a moment to soften your questions. But that's not what this book is about. My goal is to find ways to understand my guests and learn from them, not create an explosive media moment.

A more productive way to ask tough questions is to **put the words in someone else's mouth**. I learned this technique from watching Mike Wallace, who was considered one of the toughest interviewers of the twentieth century. The most cited example of his chutzpah is when he asked Iran's leader, Ayatollah Khomeini, if he was crazy.

I hunted that interview[8] down to see how he did it so I could have a model for asking challenging questions.[9] Here's what Wallace said:

"Imam, President Sadat of Egypt, a devoutly religious man, a Muslim, says that what you are doing now is—quote—'a disgrace to Islam.' And he calls you, Imam—forgive me, his words, not mine—'a lunatic.'"

Turns out Wallace didn't call Khomeini a lunatic. He cited someone else calling him that. There was a moment of friction until the translator explained that Wallace was quoting Sadat. Once that was cleared up, the conversation continued. A few minutes later, Khomeini agreed to

---

8. https://www.youtube.com/watch?v=3hX9UpCuTvo

9. Others[10] have discussed it too.

10. https://theconversation.com/
a-brief-history-of-television-interviews-and-why-live-tv-helps-those-w
ho-lie-and-want-to-hide-124471

release some of the American hostages he was holding at the time.

If I have a series of tough questions to ask my guest, I look online for examples of other people asking them. For example, I wanted to ask Ryan Hoover of the maker community Product Hunt why he didn't have enough women in his community. I did some research and found members of his own community bringing up the issue. Instead of taking a combative response, it allowed him to tell me about the partnerships he was working on to recruit a more diverse membership.

What if I can't find someone else taking the position I want to bring up? That's when I create a theoretical person. For example, when I talked with James Altucher about his self-help book, *Choose Yourself*, where he said we should be happy with who we are, something occurred to me. He's probably happy now because he's rich, not because of the techniques in his book.

I asked, "What do you say to someone listening to us thinking, 'James is only happy now because he has money in the bank. If he didn't have it, he would be right back to wrestling with his own inner demons like everyone else?'"

James acknowledged that he's happier because he's wealthy, but he talked about how he still has inner demons to deal with and uses what he wrote about to deal with them. And he said he used what's in his book when he was at rock-bottom financially and needed to climb out.

Here are a few other examples of how I phrase criticism through other people's words:

- What do you say to someone who's listening to us and thinking ...?
- What would you say to someone who thought ...?

- I imagine someone listening to us thinking ... What would you say to that?

By putting the words in someone else's mouth, you eliminate the "me versus you" feeling that comes with asking tough questions. It turns the interviewer into a partner who's working with the guest to understand. And that's where you always want to be.

But some questions are so shocking they require their own strategy. That's next.§15

15 Pre-ask the Shocking

Stun Your Audience with Audacity

What do you do when you want to ask a question so difficult, it won't cut it to just use someone else's words? Here's a technique I use to ask my toughest questions without scaring away my guests: pre-ask the shocking.

I used it when I was invited to interview investors on stage at LAUNCH Festival, the startup conference. After investor Jonathon Triest answered some of my questions about startup advice, I said to him, "You're a photographer. You weren't a startup guy. And the money you invested is family money." Then I asked him what credibility he had telling entrepreneurs how to run companies when he built his business on his family's money.

It might seem like an unfair question. But when I researched Jonathon, his family's money and his lack of entrepreneurial experience are what stood out. Anyone who knew him might wonder the same thing and feel that leaving it out was avoiding a big, obvious issue.

The challenge with asking threatening questions like this is that the interviewee can feel so insulted that they stop trying to give helpful, interesting answers. Then the interview becomes painful for the audience to sit through—not to mention you.

But Jonathon didn't close up. Instead, he looked at the audience as he gestured toward me and said, "He's a wonderful, wonderful dude."

Why? Because I tipped him off before the interview started. I explained to him that audience members who looked him up might wonder if he was just a "trust fund kid." Would he mind if I asked him about it so he could address it? He said he wouldn't mind at all. He agreed that it was worth bringing up.

And when I asked him onstage, with conference goers watching, he complimented me. Then he explained that he was a photographer, but when he worked for *Sports Illustrated*, he realized he was "a terrible sports photographer." That led him to design and to launching a design agency, which gave him entrepreneurial experience. He explained that yes, his first investment fund came out of "the dear generosity of my family." He went on to say, "I used that fund to learn the ropes, and it was a remarkable leg up. But I had to build a network. And I had to build a brand." He had the experience. Then he raised an investment fund based on his own experience, network, and credibility.

When I **pre-ask the shocking** questions before an interview, guests don't ask me to back off. Because I tell them ahead of time, they trust me more. And by explaining to them why I want to bring up the question, they understand and encourage me to do it.

◇ CAUTION   This technique is for topics that could be controversial or potentially damaging to someone's reputation—and it could be *your* reputation that's hurt if you fail to use it. Here's a quick example of a time I *didn't* pre-ask a difficult question and paid the price.

As part of my prep for an interview with an entrepreneur, I read court papers from a lawsuit he had with his ex-girlfriend. I wanted to understand his financial business acumen. The suit was written up in newspapers, so I thought it was okay to ask about it in an interview. When I brought it up, the conversation turned from how he built his business into more of an argument. We went back and forth about whether what I asked was relevant, and I couldn't get us back on track. Unable to move past it, I thanked him for doing the interview and ended it.

If I'd brought up the lawsuit beforehand and told him why I wanted to cover it, he could have declined. Or we could have come up with guidelines that would have made him feel comfortable enough to give me some useful answers.

At the very least, he wouldn't have felt blindsided.

If you have challenging questions that you want to bring up to a guest, I recommend pre-asking them before the interview. In my experience, most guests are willing, if not eager, to use interviews as a place to share their side of tough issues. And if you tip them off, they'll trust you even more with those questions.

16 "A Time When You ..."

Draw Out Interesting Stories

A lot of advice can sound cliché. But when you share advice through stories, it becomes memorable and actionable.

When I interviewed Brad Feld, an entrepreneur turned investor, he told me that business is a series of successes and failures. That's a fact, but it seems so obvious that it doesn't have much impact on an audience.

I needed a story. So I followed up with, "Can you give an example of that?"

Brad said he invested in the startup BeMANY. After a strong effort to grow it, the founder, George Jankovic, "got to the point where the business simply wasn't working."

As the biggest investor in the business, Brad said to him, "Is it worth a year of your life to keep working on this business just to get back to a place where, maybe, if you reinvent yourself, it'll be successful? Or is that opportunity cost—a year of your life—worthwhile?"

Brad then told Jankovic to turn off his phone, take his new wife to dinner, and just give himself time to think. When he got back to Brad, he decided to close the business.

After that, Jankovic raised money to buy NutriSystem, the diet company that hit on hard times. By improving its marketing and operations, he turned the company into a $2.5B business. If he hadn't accepted failure at BeMANY, he might not have reached that level of success.

I'd bet that long after you finish reading this book, that story will stay with you.

I recorded Brad's interview with a live audience watching me online. As soon as we finished, Christoph, the founder of an outsourcing company I worked with, called me. He said, "Andrew, I've been struggling with this company for a long time, and it's not working. I think it's time for me to leave Central America, go home to Europe, and start over."

We lost touch after that call, but a few years later, he found himself in San Francisco. I invited him to my house for Scotch. As we sat down, he told me his new company was doing well financially, and now he's leading a chapter of EO, a group of entrepreneurs whose businesses do over $1M per year.

Christoph told me that people said he should close down his last company, but hearing my interview with Brad convinced him.

That's the power of a good story.

So how do we get people to share their stories? I used to try asking, "Could you tell me a story?" Smart people often dismissed that request. Stories sound like what you tell two-year-olds, not how you talk to a smart audience. Those that didn't dismiss the need for stories often froze because coming up with a story is too much pressure.

I learned to rephrase my request. Instead of "could you tell me a story about that?" I used phrases like the following:

- "Tell me about a time when you did that."
- "Do you have an example of that?"
- "Tell me about the day you signed the agreement to sell your company."
- "Take me to the moment you quit. What did you say?"

Notice that I don't ask, "Tell me about the most important time …" Asking people "most" questions like this dis-
tracts them from the conversation, as you'll see in the next
section.[§17]

Take the pressure off your guest by asking for *one* story.
Any story. It doesn't have to be the pinnacle of their life,
but more often than not, the story they remember and
share with you is one of their best. If your guest can't think
of an example, share one of your own. It allows you to
model what you want them to do.

That's what I did with Allie Magyar, founder of the
events platform HUBB. I wanted to understand how one
of her childhood difficulties shaped her. She knew she had
some but couldn't think of any. So I told her about the time
when my brother fell when we were kids. With onlookers
watching, my father whispered to my brother, "We don't
have health insurance." My dad said that since we couldn't
go to a doctor, he'd need to recover on his own. I told Allie
that seeing how finances could compromise health pushed
me to earn enough money as an adult to never let it be an
impediment in my life.

That triggered something in Allie. She told me about
the time in her childhood when her dynamic, successful
dad had a drug and alcohol problem. The family finances
suffered. Still, she wanted a popsicle, so her mom gave her
the last dollar they had. It was a windy day when she acci-
dentally dropped the dollar, and it got swept away. Her
mom was reduced to tears. Money was scarce. So they
chased the dollar down till Allie got it back.

She went on to explain that that's how she runs her
company now. She said, "I still manage a budget like my
dollar is flying down the hallway."

Compare that poignant popsicle story with the answers most business people want to give. They'll share flat statements like "I like to manage my company's money well." It isn't nearly as memorable or impactful as a good story.

Seek out **specific and interesting stories** in your interviews. Pay attention when your interviewees make general statements about their lives, and follow them up with a request for specific examples.

If they say, "I like to celebrate my wins and failures," you can say, "Tell me about *a time* you celebrated a failure."

If they say, "Remembering my past successes helps me get past my current challenges," you can ask, "What's *a past success* that you think about often?"

If they tell you, "I still turn to my mom for help," you can ask, "What's *a problem* you turned to your mom for help with as an adult?"

Key insights do nothing for your audience if no one remembers them. Use stories to make them stick.

17 Stop Asking "Most" Questions

Avoid Interviewers' Worst Questions

Many folks that offer interview advice to new podcasters include lists of questions to ask guests. These lists are often packed with what I call "most" questions:

- What book had the most influence on you?
- What's the worst thing that happened to you?
- Who was the most helpful person in your life?

I see what the writers are going for. They know that interviewers have a limited time with guests, and they want to maximize that time by focusing on the biggest, best, and most significant aspects of guests' lives.

The problem with this approach is that it freezes people. It forces them to do too much mental work for too little payoff.

Take that last question, "Who was the most influential person in your life?" Your guest has to first define what "influential" means to her. Then she has to make a mental list of people who influenced her. Then she has to identify the person who was *most* influential. Then, after she comes up with an answer, she might wonder if she might insult someone she didn't pick. Would Mom feel bad, for example, if she picked Dad?

Meanwhile, as an interviewer, you probably don't need the person at the top of their list. You're just trying to understand one of their influences. So why not simply ask, "Could you tell me about someone who had a big influence on your life?"

Not only will your guest be able to answer the question more quickly, but there's a good chance this softer approach will lead to the most influential person anyway. Without the pressure on your guest to name the single most important person in their life, they will feel freer to talk to you.

Well-meaning people make this mistake in daily life all the time. When I finished backpacking around Europe, I got off the plane and went straight to my friend's home for dinner. Their first question was one that I was asked by others for weeks after I returned: what was your favorite city?

I wasn't sure. Was it Pamplona, where I ran with the bulls? Paris, where I sat in outdoor cafes and quietly journaled for days? Or one of the dozens of other cities? So I said, "It was all amazing."

Was I overthinking it? Of course.

I eventually realized they just wanted to hear about my trip, so I'd say, "I'm not sure which is my favorite, but one of them was ..." and tell a story from my trip.

As an interviewer, I don't want to count on people making that leap. So I usually rephrase all **"most" questions** in a way that gives guests options. Instead of asking "Who's the most important person you hired?" I go with "Who's an important person you hired?"

There are exceptions to this rule. For example, when I ask a founder what their top source for customers is, I don't want to hear about the third most effective channel. I'm trying to understand what's working best. It's a factual piece of information that founders should know the answer to, so that's what I ask for.

We're taught to seek out click-baity answers to complex questions. In reality, the lives of our guests are much more nuanced. Don't put them on the spot by asking "most" questions. Give them the opportunity to explore your question and answer it with the depth it deserves.

18 Use Double-Barreled Questions

How to Ask Questions You Shouldn't Ask

I have a simple way to get relative strangers to talk to me about their parents, sex lives, and other personal topics.

I can almost hear you say, "That seems inappropriate, Andrew." So first I need you to understand *why* I do it. Then I'll show you how.

Years ago, I pressed Alexis Ohanian, co-founder of Reddit, to help me understand the business rationale behind selling his company so early. Today Reddit is worth over $6B, but he sold it for $10M–$20M.

Despite my efforts, I couldn't get an answer that made sense to me.

Then, sometime after my interview, Alexis wrote a blog post where he shared the truth. There were family issues that influenced his decision to sell Reddit. I finally understood. Not all business decisions are made for business reasons. We're human. The personal side matters.

But how could I ask about the personal side without sounding nosy or unprofessional?

My solution came from a conversation I had with the investigative reporter, John Sawatsky. He told me that he warns reporters *not* to ask what he called "double-barreled questions."

Double-barreled questions are questions that address two different issues. When reporters ask double-barreled questions, their subjects answer the easy part and ignore the part they don't like.

Ask a politician in a tight race, "Should people burn the American flag, and would you put them in jail for doing it?" and they might launch into why burning the flag is wrong and completely ignore the thornier issue of punishing people who do it.

As I thought about it, I realized double-barreled questions could be my key to bringing up personal issues.

Unlike a reporter, I *want* to give my interviewees an out from answering a question if it makes them uncomfortable. If I'm wondering whether someone got a divorce, instead of asking "did you get a divorce?" and making a business conversation feel uncomfortably personal, I might ask, "Do you feel comfortable saying if you divorced your husband?"

Break that down, and you'll see I'm actually asking two questions:

1. Are you divorced?
2. Do you feel comfortable talking about it?

People who don't feel comfortable answering the divorce question will answer the easy question: no, I do not feel comfortable.

Here are a few actual examples from my interviews:

Example One: *Is it inappropriate for me to ask you if you're a millionaire now because of this business?*

Answer: *I didn't become a millionaire from the business.*

Example Two: *Is it inappropriate to ask if [your partner] gets half of this business?*

Answer: *He doesn't own half my business.*

Example Three: *Is it inappropriate for me to ask you who you're dating these days?*

Answer: *I'm dating my business ideas and my fifty-six thousand books.*

The double-barreled question is so transformational that I use them outside of interviews often. When I'm out with my wife and she hears a double-barreled question come out of my mouth, she smiles. She knows there's a good chance the stranger we just met will share a personal experience they hardly ever share. And with that, the stranger will instantly become a close friend.

To be clear, this technique isn't fool-proof. It doesn't always get people to open up, and that's the point. The double-barreled approach gives people an easy out to avoid topics that are too personal for them. As an interviewer, be prepared to move on quickly if your guest opts out of the question.

Here's an example of when an interviewee didn't want to get personal. Toward the end of my conversation with Mikkel Svane, the founder of customer service software,

Zendesk, we talked about the challenges of his early days in business. Then I tried to get more personal.

> **Me:** *Is it inappropriate for me to ask you if you're still with your wife?*

> **Mikkel:** *Yes, it's highly inappropriate.*

So I didn't press. We moved on.

Instead, I shared something personal from my life about the difficulty of working hard after college while others my age were having fun. Then I quickly shifted the conversation to a book he mentioned he liked.

When I watch the video of that conversation years later, I can see discomfort in his face when I tried to talk about his family. When I shifted to my story, he smiled a bit, and when I switched to the book discussion, his face lit up. It all happened in under 60 seconds because I didn't linger on a topic he told me to avoid.

That's what this technique is about. We want to give people a way to get personal if they're comfortable doing it, but also give them a graceful way to move past it if they aren't.

19 Use Icon Stories

Recruit Their Heroes to Help You

Entrepreneurs are scrappy by nature. But not everyone sees this as a positive trait.

I've been criticized for the way I funded my first internet company. When no investor would bet on me, I called up J.Crew and asked, "Can I return all the clothes I bought when I was at New York University?"

The rep said, "Yes. We have a lifetime return policy."

"Are you sure? I wore clothes throughout college. And I took the subway to school."

She said, "Gladly. That's our policy."

So I mailed back all my old J.Crew clothes and got a few thousand dollars to start my company. The business generated over $30M in sales. I've been a loyal customer of J.Crew ever since.

When I published my story a few years back, entrepreneurs praised my hustle. But I also got the kind of criticism and insults that most people try to avoid.

This negative response is why some of my interviewees are hesitant to share their craftiest growth tactics. Still, as an interviewer, it's my job to uncover those types of lessons. Otherwise, I would be sharing an incomplete picture with my audience. Without knowing the full story behind people's success, we risk frustration and shame from attempting to be like them and falling short.

So how could I get guests to open up about topics they were reluctant to discuss in public? My solution was to use **icon stories** to destigmatize those topics by drawing comparisons to their heroes.

Software entrepreneurs admire Matt Mullenweg, the founder of WordPress, because more than a third of websites are built with his software. But people are often shocked to learn that in the early days, Matt spammed websites to grow his business. As he explained in our interview, Matt went to blogs he liked and pitched his software in the comments.

Now, when I sense that a software founder isn't sharing the full story of how they grew, I tell them how Matt got his first customers. By sharing Matt's story, it takes the stigma out of it.

You can see this technique in action in my interview with Emmanuel Straschnov, creator of Bubble, the no-code app builder. When I asked him how he got his first customers, he talked about creating a community. My research showed the community he built was robust. But I wanted to learn a non-obvious way he landed customers, so I told him about Matt spamming. His response? "So I used to do that. I did that in the first two, three years when the product was not good enough." Then he talked about why it didn't work for him and gave us a deeper understanding of how he grew his company.

I'm always on the lookout for iconic stories like Matt's. I write them down to help me remember to use them in my interviews. When I heard that investor Paul Graham said, "Startups often have to do slightly devious things," I knew I spotted a helpful quote. When describing the investment philosophy for his firm, Y Combinator, Graham said, "We're not looking for people who did what they were told in life." I wrote that down too.

I use Paul's lines in pre-interview conversations. They give me a quick way to show an upcoming guest that it's OK to reveal the "slightly devious things" it takes to succeed. In fact, it's preferable.

We'll cover the pre-interview process in the next part.[§24] But first, I want to share another use for these icon stories—they help reassure a guest after they reveal something they might later regret.

You can see this in my interview with Ilya Lichtenstein, founder of the ad data platform MixRank. He told me a great story from the early days of his company. To get customers, he wrote a script that collected images from other successful online ads and gave them to his prospects to use for their ads. He copied thousands of businesses' ad creatives *en masse* and used them to grow his company.

"Is that a potential copyright violation?" I asked.

He admitted it was "skirting the line."

When a CEO of a data company says that, it presents a few dangers to the interview. The most immediate one is that he'll clam up and stop revealing more. But there's also a danger that the audience might turn against him. Both of those outcomes are anathema to my goal of sharing how founders *really* build their companies. So I followed up his answer by repeating Paul's quote about being devious. Ilya responded, "Yeah, I think that falls into the slightly devious category." The conversation moved on, and the audience's reaction was positive.

If you're trying to create an atmosphere where your interviewees can reveal the hidden parts of themselves, show them how their idols did it. When you come across a quote or story that illustrates it, keep it handy.

20 "Sorry to Interrupt ..."

Smoothly Cut Off Guests without Offense

I thought he'd be livid.

After months of convincing an entrepreneur to come onto *Mixergy* for an interview, I spent much of the conversation interrupting him. Talk about a terrible host, right?

But I had to do it. He was going on and on and taking us off-track. I couldn't let my listeners put up with that. So I interrupted him—quite a bit.

After the interview, I prepared for him to rip into me.

Instead, he said, "Thanks for getting me back on track. I'm not good at public speaking. I found myself droning on and didn't know how to get back to my point. I can see why my friends like being interviewed by you. You're good."

Interruptions are considered a cardinal sin of polite society. But when done right, they not only improve your conversations—they also make your counterpart look better in the process. When people struggle to get a point across, they start to talk in circles. Instead of clarifying, they make their point *less clear* with each round of explanations. Most people, like my interview guest, will appreciate your help sounding competent.

So how did I interrupt this entrepreneur without being rude or embarrassing him? I wasn't exactly sure how I did it myself. So I examined the transcript.

Turns out, I stumbled upon a surprisingly simple solution—a short phrase that exonerated me from any breach of conversation etiquette:

"I'm sorry to interrupt, but ..."

Then I'd complete the sentence by explaining *why* I was interrupting and often citing my higher purpose.

I don't know where I learned this technique, but I used it for years without realizing it. Searching through my 2,100+ transcripts, I discovered more than 170 instances of me saying "I'm sorry to interrupt."

I'll refrain from calling out any particular entrepreneurs in this section. Instead, here are some examples to show you just how effective this magical little phrase can be:

> *I'm sorry to interrupt, but I really want to get into the details of this.*
>
> *I'm sorry to interrupt, but [you said] "fanatical optimism." How do you maintain fanatical optimism?*
>
> *I'm sorry to interrupt, but I really want to understand this concept because ...*
>
> *I'm sorry to interrupt, but this is something that I need to learn from you ...*
>
> *I'm sorry to interrupt, but I want to talk more in depth about that ...*

Don't get me wrong—interrupting someone does not feel natural to most people. It will make you feel rude and awkward at first. You're doing something every teacher and authority figure taught you not to do.

A **"sorry to interrupt"** moment is when you interrupt and share *why* you're interrupting. People won't think you're rude—they'll think you're considerate. If you're interrupting for a meaningful reason, your guest will appreciate it.

Not every interruption is created equal. Saying "sorry to interrupt, but you're boring me" is extremely rude and will lose you a friend or colleague. On the other hand, "sorry to interrupt, but I really want to make sure I understand what you're saying" is flattering and will win you a fan for life.

21 Avoid Train Crashes

How to Recover from a Nervous Mistake

A few years ago, I helped a few dozen members of my audience start interviewing. In a weekly meeting, one of them said, "I worry about not paying attention to my interviewee's answer and being stuck finding a way to respond." That's much more common than people realize because many interviewers edit those goofs out.

I was sweating when that happened to me in my interview with Mike Jones, an entrepreneur who sold his company to AOL. My audience, at the time, was limited to the small Los Angeles tech community, where everyone knew Mike as one of its most successful members. I felt pressure to get the interview right.

To do that, I put together pages of notes. Then I took more notes during our conversation because I think better when I take notes. At one point, while he answered my question, I tried to find a note, but it was lost in the pages floating around on my desk. I didn't hear his answer to my question. He paused. It was my turn to talk.

What could I do? If he had said something poignant and I shot back an irrelevant question, I'd seem insensitive. If I admitted I didn't pay attention, I could lose credibility. I paused for a moment and suddenly came up with a question that I felt would always be relevant: "What's your motivation?" Then I explained that I admired the hard work he put in, years after selling his company. Why was he putting himself through it?

It worked. Why? Because I genuinely wonder what motivates all my guests. And it's a question I feel is relevant no matter what my guests say. If they tell me about something painful they did, it makes sense to ask "what's your motivation?" so I could understand why they put themselves through the difficulty. If they tell me about something heroic, "what's your motivation?" fits too. If they tell me about their childhood, "what's your motivation?" can be a good follow-up.

In the early days, I got stuck like that often because I was still nervous. So I kept the "what's your motivation?" question in the back of my mind and used it as needed.

If you're ever stuck, find your own "in case of emergency" questions. Here are some examples:

- Listening to you, I can see you work hard. I have to pause and ask: what's your motivation?
- Before we continue, I want to check in: how is this interview going for you?
- I hate to switch gears, but with so little time together, I have to ask you about …

And if you have more guts than I did when I started, go with, "I'm sorry. I'm so new at this that I was overly worried about my notes and missed what you said."

Like all things in life, it's okay to make mistakes while interviewing. What's important is that you recover and keep going.

22 Home Run Questions

End on a High Note

One day, as I was leaving my office, I got a call from a prominent Silicon Valley founder I interviewed earlier that morning.

"I'm upset with you," she came right out and said.

I was stunned. I racked my brain trying to figure out why she'd be mad. Her interview went off without a hitch. If anything, I felt like I was *more* accommodating than usual. She was in a relationship with someone famous. To preserve her privacy, I didn't bring it up, even though it could have given my show a traffic boost. We focused strictly on her business, and I even let her promote more than I normally would.

My only tough question came at the end. We had scheduled the interview multiple times, and she didn't show up. She seemed to have done that to another interviewer, who mentioned it on his podcast. So I asked why she didn't show up when she said she would.

She apologized and explained how overbooked she was lately—totally understandable for a founder of her stature. I thanked her, closed out the interview, and thought nothing of it.

Apparently, she thought of nothing *but* that last question.

I asked one tough question. Just one. And I waited until we had built enough rapport for me to bring it up. Why did that make her upset? She was both a listener of mine and a paying customer. She knew I liked to have deeper, more meaningful conversations than most interviewers were willing to risk. This question was a softball by my standards.

Why?

My interview coach read the transcript from our interview and quickly identified the problem: I violated the peak-end rule.

The **peak-end rule** is a cognitive bias that affects the way we recall events. Humans tend to remember two aspects of an experience more than anything else: the peak (i.e., most intense) and the end.

By saving my toughest question for last, I unwittingly stacked the peak and the end into one dramatic moment. It was the only thing my guest remembered from our talk. No wonder she was upset.

Up until that moment, I always saved my toughest questions for the end. I wanted to close out the interview with something memorable for my audience. I thought my interviewee would trust me enough to know my intentions were good. After receiving that call from my upset guest, I realized she probably wasn't the only one. Other guests might have been hurt by my actions too—they just didn't tell me.

But it wasn't just the peak-end rule that was working against me. Saving the hardest questions for last invoked an even more primal emotion: vulnerability.

I once listened to Oprah Winfrey being interviewed at Stanford University, where she shared some behind-the-scenes details of her famous talk show. She said that throughout her storied career, each of her guests would ask the same question after the interview: "Was that OK?"

Barack Obama and George Bush both asked the question. Beyoncé, who taught Winfrey how to twerk on live TV, also asked. Even the most seasoned public figures feel vulnerable after a performance. Asking a tough question at the end was like a punch to their confidence before saying goodbye.

I decided to stop saving my gutsiest questions for last. I would ask those somewhere in the middle and then end the conversation with something easy.

My goal was to give my guests a **home run question** they could knock out of the park and leave the interview feeling confident about their performance.

But I didn't stop there. I started anticipating my guests' need for validation. When an interview ended, I thanked them, told them they did well, and mentioned one specific thing I liked from our conversation.

Before I made this adjustment, guests would routinely ask me to give them another chance to record their interviews. "I think I could have done better," they'd say. "How about we record again next week?"

I saw a drastic reduction in these requests by ending interviews on a home run question. Guests started feeling happy and confident after our interviews instead of vulnerable and regretful.

As an interviewer, it takes nothing to end your conversations on a high note. But for your guests, it means everything.

23 The Talking Release

Remember This above All

Before we leave this section, I want to leave you with one important message: if you fail with every tip I gave you so far, you'll do well if you simply let your guest talk.

I realized the importance of this years ago at a quiet dinner with my brother, Michael. I got a call from one of the employees at the greeting card company he and I founded.

"Andrew, I can't stop crying," she said.

I was surprised, not that she was crying or the reason *why* she was crying. I knew about the tough breakup she was going through. What took me by surprise was that she wanted to talk to *me*, not Michael.

Ever since we were kids, people brought their business questions to me and their personal issues to Michael. Even adults would open up to Michael when we were barely teenagers.

But maybe our employee had noticed all the work I'd done to improve my relationship skills.

"My ex is being intentionally cruel," she sobbed. "He keeps flaunting his new relationships. He wants me to be jealous."

"Don't let him do this to you," I said, trying to show that I empathized. Then I gave her some advice.

She stopped responding. I sensed that I'd lost her. I could tell this wasn't what she needed, but I didn't know why.

She thanked me, and we hung up.

Then Michael's phone rang. She'd called him. I guess she didn't realize we were at dinner together, and she looked to him for help.

I sat silently, listening, trying to understand what magic he had. I wanted to understand what I should have said.

Here's his magic. He asked what happened. Then he didn't say much more than "mhmm" for a long time. He followed that by asking "why did you say that?" and went back to listening.

When they hung up, I asked my brother, "How's she doing now?" He told me she was feeling better. She already knew not to let her ex get under her skin and to ignore him, but it still bothered her. After unloading on Michael, she felt better.

That's the magic of listening. People prefer to be heard than to be helped.

I used to wonder why some interviewees spoke to me when my audience was tiny in comparison to their reach. What did they get out of it? I found my answer after interviewing one of the most well-known bloggers of the day, Brian Clark of Copyblogger, about how he turned his site into a $7M-per-year software company.

When we were done, he exhaled and told me that it was good for him to take a pause from the business and think about how he built it and what he stood for. It made him a better leader to remember. It's not what I said that helped him. It's what he remembered and told me. I've since experienced the same thing while being interviewed by new podcasters, speaking to high school students, and even writing this book.

Listening is a critical skill for an interviewer, even while off the air. A few years after I started interviewing, our producer Jeremy Weisz texted me, "Andrew, the founder you interviewed yesterday is furious. He asked us not to publish the interview and won't change his mind."

Remembering what I learned from Michael, I called the founder. "I heard you weren't happy with the interview I recorded with you," I said. Then I let him talk. He vented that he didn't come across well.

I wanted to explain to him that he did well, but I resisted the urge. Instead, I simply asked, "Why?"

He told me he knew my podcast was listened to by people who might fund his company or do business with him in the future, and he wanted it to be as good as possible.

"What didn't you like about it?" I asked. He explained that he said "um" and "uh" too much. He thought it made him sound like he didn't know what he was talking about.

One of the biggest complaints I get from people I interview is "I said 'um' too many times." Successful entrepreneurs who have no trouble telling me that part of a startup's job is to be OK with publishing software before it's perfect will beat themselves up for saying "um." It pains me to see how upset they get over saying something that's actually helpful. Filler words add a feeling of authenticity, because we all use them.

Though our editing software, Descript, has a simple way of removing filler words, I don't use it. Eliminating all "flaws" is a mistake. It makes people sound fake. It reminds me of photographers who use Photoshop to edit away "flaws" and end up with photos of women who have no knees.

I didn't tell him any of that. I used what I learned from Michael. I let this founder complain. I only asked questions to help understand what he was going through. After venting, he said, "Publish the interview or not. It's up to you. I just feel that I could have done better. It wasn't bad, but I think I could do better."

I published it. The audience loved the interview. But I couldn't have published it if I hadn't given him time to vent. To be heard.

PART II: PREPARING FOR INTERVIEWS

In Part I, you learned high-impact conversation techniques that will elevate every interaction and interview. But great conversations are created before they even begin. If you're ready to uncover deeper insights from your guests and people you admire, it's time to learn how to prepare for each interview.

Preparation is what separates the great interviewers from the good ones. It's also why some people can walk into a room and immediately make a deep connection with everyone they meet. In this part, we'll take a step back and look at the interview process as a whole. We'll start with teaching you how pre-interviewing will improve your conversations. Then we'll look at five different interview structures you can use to organize your conversation. After that, I'll share how I conduct research on my interviewees.

Finally, we'll close with a few more techniques to keep conversations meaningful and interesting.

24 Pre-interview

Prep Guests for Excellence

The pre-interview is an underappreciated part of the interview process because it's hidden from the audience. But if you spend even a few minutes doing it, your interview will be noticeably better.

I added pre-interviews to my process to fix a common problem: guests forgetting to share their most memorable stories.

After recording one of my first interviews, I saw my guest exhale and let out the pressure he built up. "You did great," I said.

"Thanks, but I wish I told you the story of how I got my first customers. I found a way to automate posting my ads on dozens of Craigslist sites. It violated their rules, but it helped my company take off. I forgot about it when you asked me. When I remembered, the conversation felt too far along to return to it."

That disappointed me. I started interviewing to understand how founders really built their companies. I hated missing defining moments like that. And I kept missing them. It makes sense—people under pressure can be forgetful.

I needed to find a way to solve this problem for my guests. I wondered, how did major TV shows handle this issue?

Then I remembered watching *The Larry Sanders Show*, an HBO sitcom loved by talk show producers because of how accurately and hilariously it depicted their jobs. In episode after episode, I watched Larry Sanders' producers trying to cajole reluctant comedians to sit for a pre-interview.

If TV producers (even fictional ones) thought pre-interviews were that important for professional performers, maybe they would help with my guests too.

I decided to try a pre-interview. I knew my guests had limited time and wouldn't get on a call with me unless I explained why they needed to do it. I emailed one of my interviewees. "We should talk. Your interview is going to live online forever and will be found by future employees, investors, etc. I want to make sure you sound good. Would you call me so I could go over what I'll ask in your interview?"

An hour later, while I was driving, he called. I pulled over and did my first pre-interview. I asked him the questions I planned to ask in the interview and helped him remember his experiences. If a response was too general, I pushed for one that was more specific. If he couldn't remember an experience, I gave him more quiet space to think.

Out of respect for my guest's time and mine, I used my interrupting technique more often than in an actual interview. (See the previous section[20] on how to do that.) As soon as I noticed that he had a good story to share, I cut him off. "To keep it sounding fresh at our interview, let's hold the rest of the story," I said. Then I moved on to the next question.

Let me say that again: pre-interviews can backfire on you if you don't cut off your guests' stories. If I let a guest tell their full story in the pre-interview, they will hesitate to repeat themselves in the actual interview. It's like they're afraid of boring me, so I either get a severely shortened, less interesting version of the story, or no story at all.

During the pre-interview, I take notes on the stories my guest told well. This helps me trigger those stories at key moments in the interview. I also make a note of the stories that were too convoluted and should stay out of the interview.

Pre-interviews are a powerful tool that help my guests remember the most important details of their lives and share them clearly. Often, when a listener asks me how I got a guest to open up about a tough topic, it's because I helped them get comfortable by talking about it in private first.

Over the years, my responsibilities have grown to include selling ads, finding guests, and building a membership site. I eventually reached a point where I couldn't run *Mixergy* on my own, so I hired Arie Desormeaux, a full-time producer, to take over pre-interviewing. I started asking interviewees to schedule calls with her before booking their interviews.

My goal was to save time, but I quickly realized a bigger benefit. Having another perspective improves the quality of the pre-interview. I grew up in New York, where bluntness and speed were prized. Arie has a softer touch, so guests open up to her. A founder once told me that he cried in his pre-interview. I immediately texted Arie and asked why she hadn't told me.

"Oh, it happens too often for me to keep telling you."

If you recruit a pre-interviewer, look for someone whose style compliments yours in the way Arie's compliments mine. If you're fast and direct like me, look for someone who's more deliberate. If you're more focused on facts, look for someone who's curious about the emotional aspects of your guests' stories.

If you don't have a team, you might be tempted to send over a list of questions before the interview. I found that shortcut to be much less effective. Most guests will skim the list and move on—some won't even do that.

In some cases, sending over questions ahead of time can give the guest false confidence. I learned this lesson the hard way when I interviewed the head of a PR agency. Because our time zones made coordination difficult, I let her skip the pre-interview. Before the interview started, she said my questions helped her prepare. Then, to my surprise, she stammered through the entire conversation. She couldn't even remember details like how she got her first customers. (If anything, this struggle was an ode to her success—she had been in business a long time.)

Still, I wondered why sending the questions ahead of time didn't help. When the interview was over, I got my answer. She read the questions and saw they were about her life and business, which she understood better than anyone. She assumed she'd know the answers and didn't take the time to prepare herself.

If you can't do a pre-interview ahead of time, spend a few minutes with your guest before the interview starts. Use that time to do a mini pre-interview. Say something like, "Before we record, I have a few questions that I'd like some clarification on." Then ask just the key questions. Move through your questions as quickly as possible. Remember to gently interrupt long stories, even if they're good. Explain to your guest that you want the stories to sound fresh in the interview.

Don't assume your guests will be prepared. Don't let them make that assumption either. Spend some time with your guest to discuss their stories and experience. It'll make for a better interview for you, your audience, and your interviewee.

Tips for Pre-interviewing

- Most people aren't familiar with pre-interviews, so explain what you're going to do and why. This is especially important if you're doing the pre-interview yourself. You don't want your guest to confuse it with the actual interview.

- Focus on the key parts of the interview. This isn't a dry run of the interview—it's information gathering, or as I like to call it, story gathering.

- If you're doing the pre-interview yourself, always interrupt good stories and explain that you want your guest to sound unrehearsed and fresh in the interview.

- The output of a successful pre-interview is a list of stories your guest tells well and maybe a few that you should stay away from.

25 Interview Structure 1: Hero's Journey

Throughout human history, knowledge has been passed down from generation to generation. Not with charts and spreadsheets, but with stories.

Stories have a way of embedding lessons into our minds. They help us remember hard-earned wisdom we'd otherwise forget. That's why, as an interviewer, my goal is to get guests to tell me stories from their lives—not just share what they've learned.

The quintessential human story is what Joseph Campbell dubbed the Hero's Journey. But before we get into that, let me tell you a story of my own.

Shortly after starting my first company—an online greeting card business—I was struggling to make sales. Banner ads were an important part of my business model, but I didn't have the chops to convince sponsors to take a chance on my site. That's when I learned about Rosalind Resnick, a seasoned entrepreneur whose company sold ads for online businesses. I thought, if I could just get Rosalind to help me, my business might survive.

So I called her office. Then I called again. And again. But every time I called, I was turned down because my company was too small. I offered to split my revenue with them 50/50. No dice. I tried everything to persuade them to work with me. Finally, one of the sales reps politely asked me to stop calling.

But I was desperate. My company was on the verge of folding, and I needed ad revenue yesterday. So I tried something different. Instead of calling, I showed up to

Rosalind's office unannounced. I found Rosalind and handed her a check for $2,000, which was all the money I had left in my bank account. I said, "I know you think we're too small, but I guarantee that if we work together, we'll both make money."

Rosalind was surprised, to say the least. But I continued. "Take this check, and if you ever doubt I'm worth working with, you can cash it and make an easy $2,000."

At that point, Rosalind told her team to start working with my company immediately. We went on to make millions of dollars together, and she gave me back that check, uncashed.

Where did I learn to make such a bold move? I struggled to recall. It certainly didn't come from any business class. But then I remembered a biography I read as a kid. It was about Ted Turner, the legendary TV mogul. Before Ted was "Ted," he had to make bold gestures to get his channels on cable television. In one instance, he barged into the office of cable giant, Telecommunications Inc., and offered to kiss the feet of its CEO.

I didn't take notes while reading Ted's story, but it got stuck in my brain and became part of how I thought. Without realizing it, I emulated Ted Turner to help my startup survive. These are the types of life-changing stories I want my interview guests to share with my audience.

Great interviewers are great storytellers. They lead their guests—along with the audience—on a journey of adventure, struggle, rebirth, and triumph. In other words, the best interviewers follow the Hero's Journey.

The Hero's Journey looks like this:

1. A person we care about—our hero.
2. The hero faces a problem or opportunity worth pursuing.

3. They start their journey.
4. Inevitably, the hero hits an obstacle.
5. They find help from an aid or mentor.
6. The hero improves and starts to succeed.
7. But then a major battle emerges. The hero falls into an abyss.
8. The only way to survive is to transform, so our hero becomes someone new.
9. The transformation leads our hero to victory and self-actualization.

The Hero's Journey is my go-to interviewing framework. Here's how I map questions to each stage of the journey, along with hypothetical answers I might receive:

1. A person we care about—our hero.

   - **Question:** What were you doing before you started your company?
   - **Answer:** I worked at a bank. I hated it. I used to listen to entrepreneurship podcasts, wishing I could do something like that, but I couldn't do it. My family always had financial problems when I was growing up, and I wanted safety.

2. The hero faces a problem or opportunity worth pursuing.

   - **Question:** What led you to start your business?
   - **Answer:** Then the 2008 financial crisis hit. My boss said to me, "You do a good job, but we can't afford to keep you."

3. They start their journey.

   - **Question:** How did you deal with losing your job?

- **Answer:** I tried to find a job, but no one was hiring. So I decided to try starting my own online business. I was always into journaling, so I created my own journal and sold it online.

4. Inevitably, the hero hits an obstacle.

    - **Question:** Did you sell a lot of journals at first?
    - **Answer:** No, I didn't sell any. I couldn't get anyone to come to my site.

5. They find help from an aid or mentor.

    - **Question:** How did you learn to sell?
    - **Answer:** I met an entrepreneur who figured out search engine optimization, SEO. He wrote blog posts using keywords that Google searchers were looking for. I didn't have enough money to buy ads, but I had plenty of time, so I started doing what he showed me.

6. The hero improves and starts to succeed.

    - **Question:** How did you finally get sales?
    - **Answer:** SEO took a few months, but eventually, I got customers. People searching for phrases like "journal ideas" and "how to start a journal" would see my site in the search results, click over to read my blog posts, and often buy one of my journals. The writing was pretty bad, but it worked on Google's algorithms.

7. But then a major battle emerges. The hero falls into an abyss.

    - **Question:** So after that it was easy?

- **Answer:** No. I was too dependent on Google. They changed their search algorithm, and almost all my traffic disappeared, instantly. By then, the economy had improved, and I considered going back to look for a job, even though I knew it would make me feel dead inside to live that way again.

8. The only way to survive is to transform, so our hero becomes someone new.

    - **Question:** Why didn't you give up on your idea?
    - **Answer:** Actually, I almost did. I got a job offer for a bit more money than I made before I got laid off. But when it was time to accept the job, I started asking myself, "Do you want to be scared your whole life?" I decided that if I figured out SEO before, I could relearn the new way. And if I could learn SEO, I could figure out how to do social media, buy ads, and do other marketing things. So I stopped thinking about a job and started obsessing over self-improvement. It took me a year to get my site's traffic back to where it was before Google's algorithm change, but I did it.

9. The transformation leads our hero to victory and self-actualization.

    - **Question:** How's your business today?
    - **Answer:** Today, I get my customers from a mix of five different places. If Google changes its algorithm again or something else shuts down, it wouldn't be the end for me. I have a real and sustainable business. I now know that everything in life is learnable. Now, when I feel I can't do something, I know that I could learn it. It's like a superpower.

No interview will follow the Hero's Journey outline perfectly, and that's OK. We're not trying to script the conversation, just guide it. For a real-life example of the Hero's Journey interview structure, listen to *Mixergy* Episode #2,122 with Andrew Gazdecki, founder of MicroAcquire.

Andrew is a startup hero in many people's eyes: humble, hardworking, and fighting for the little guys. His journey closely maps with the Hero's Journey, from a less-than-ideal upbringing to meeting a mentor, to selling his company for life-changing money. Now Andrew's on a new journey—to change the way startups are bought and sold. His story is fascinating on its own, but it's even more compelling because it follows that ancient Hero's Journey framework.

You can use the Hero's Journey framework for just about any interview, but it's not the only structure you can follow. If your goal is to help your audience learn a new skill, use the next interview structure: the how-to.

26 Interview Structure 2: How-To

Most interviewers guide their how-to interviews based on the questions they think up when they're trying to learn the topic. That approach works fine, but it's not the optimal way to teach something.

My how-to interview structure is so effective that I call those interviews "Master Classes," and I charge for them. That's because by the end of the interview, my audience will have acquired a useful new skill, like growing their website's sales. But how-to interviews also take more work to put together. I can't do these interviews well without an extensive pre-interview or doing heavy research.

In this section, I'll show you how to prepare a how-to interview that's so good, your audience will pay you to teach them. At the very least, you'll know how to structure conversations to learn more effectively from experts you admire.

Before we get into it, let's talk for a minute about Blue Apron.

Like millions of Americans, I signed up for that weekly meal kit service, which mails me ingredients and a recipe card to cook at home. Even though I never cooked before, I was so proud of what it taught me that I texted photos of my finished meals to my family.

I want my guests to lead my audience through that kind of transformation. Not only do they learn a new skill, but they can't wait to tell people about it. To do this, I model my how-to interviews after a Blue Apron recipe card.[11]

---

11. https://www.blueapron.com/pages/sample-recipes

The recipe card starts with a clear, specific name. Not "Middle Eastern Meal" or "A Healthy Meal," but "Shakshuka," an Israeli breakfast dish featuring eggs and tomatoes. A good how-to interview starts the same way—not with a generic title like "How to Grow Your Business," but "How to Grow Your Email List Using Social Media."

Not sure what shakshuka looks like? Have no fear. The recipe card also includes a high-resolution photo that gives you a clear vision of the finished product. It also helps you grasp the finer details, like how thin to slice the peppers. The same principle applies to how-to interviews. The audience needs a vision of what their future will look like if they listen to the interview. I ask my guests to share a story that illustrates the power of the lesson they're about to teach us.

When Scott Bintz, founder of RealTruck, taught a master class on creating a fun culture that grows online sales, we made sure to start with an example. He told me how his team set a goal of reaching $10M in sales. They made it fun by getting Scott to commit to buzzing his hair and donating it once they hit the goal. Now that's the kind of revenue and *esprit de corps* my audience aspires to.

I like to publish my how-to interviews with video as well as audio, so I asked Scott to show us the outcome. Scott shared a before-and-after photo of him with shoulder-length hair and then with a buzz cut. The visual makes the interview more interesting, but it also adds credibility. People believe what they see.

After understanding what the interview will teach, listeners are ready to take action.

The Blue Apron recipe card breaks up meal prep into five to eight steps. I ask my guest to do the same with their lesson by sharing each step they took to achieve the goal we promised in the interview title. If we can't boil it down to eight steps or less, we narrow the scope of the lesson. Is "How to Get Your First 100,000 Email Subscribers" too complex to do in eight steps? Fine. Then let's teach "How to Get Your First 1,000 Email Subscribers."

This point is important to repeat: When teaching your audience a new skill, make sure it fits into five to eight steps. If not, narrow the scope of the lesson until it does.

The Blue Apron recipe card also has a photo of each step. New cooks like me need to see how small "diced onions" should be, for example. I do the same with my how-to interviews. I ask for a story to illustrate each step. If a guest says, "I emailed my friends and asked them to join my email list," I ask for more details. I want to hear the story of how the guest exported his address book and stuffed all the email addresses into the BCC field of his email message. I want to hear how his high school sweetheart replied and how he wished he'd gone over his list before including her. Details like that make the story interesting and show that perfection isn't necessary.

But I also want actual visual examples when possible. If my guest says they did something, I ask them to show it to me. Did they email their friends during the product launch? Great. I ask them to please search their email app and find the message. When they find it, it'll often trigger an important memory, like how they used tracking software to see which recipients opened their email.

Some interviewees are reluctant to go this extra step and find examples from years ago. It's daunting. So, as always, I share my higher purpose. I explain that they're changing people's lives—that audience members who are most likely to take action are the ones who need specifics. I tell them that finding these visuals is useful beyond our interview too. Next time they give a speech at a conference, for example, having these visuals handy will make for a more inspiring presentation. I say that future employees will understand their company better if they see how it was built.

I'll also hunt for visuals myself. You'd be amazed by what you can find with a few searches on Google or Facebook. I also love using specialty search sites. If they refer to an ad, I'll search WhatRunsWhere,[12] a database of digital advertising. If they tell me what their site looked like years ago, I'll grab a screenshot of it from the Internet Archive.[13] Once I find the visual and show it to the guest, they realize just how committed I am to the work. They often reciprocate by doubling down on their commitment to teaching my audience.

After I have examples for each step, our outline is nearly finished. There's just one element left—one that recipe cards don't need but how-to interviews do. It's what I call the "before story."

You know how diet ads use before-and-after photos of their successful customers? It's so other people will see the dramatic difference and think, "If they can do it, I can do it." That's the message you're trying to send with the "before story."

You want your audience to understand how painful life was for your guest before they mastered what they're about to teach. The **"before story"** should be the first thing your audience hears. You want them to relate to your guest's painful past and aspire to experience the same transformation.

When Chris Ronzio, founder and CEO of Trainual, taught my audience how to systemize their companies, I asked him to share what life was like before he learned to

---

12. https://www.whatrunswhere.com/

13. https://archive.org/

take control of his businesses. He told the story of a video production company he ran, which was hired to shoot a cheerleading competition. On the day of the shoot, no one from his team showed up—the company was too disorganized to keep track of clients. That was the moment that inspired Chris to develop a world-class organization system, which eventually turned into Trainual.

The how-to interview structure is the best way to blend stories with actionable advice. But as you can see, it's not necessary for every conversation. Reserve your how-to interviews—and the effort that goes into them—for your guests with high-dollar, in-demand skills.

Example Outline: How-To Interview

Below is an actual outline my team and I created before interviewing Scott Bintz.

We based this outline on his book, *Principles to Fortune*, as well as our own research and a short pre-interview. You'll notice the outline doesn't include full stories. I just need a short prompt that will guide my guest to his story.

> **Topic: How to Create a Company Culture That Grows Sales**
>
> **Interviewee:** *Scott Bintz, founder of RealTruck, an online auto-part store*
>
> **Before:** *Scott's story about how he started to hate working at the company he founded and led. He tried creating a company culture by writing down the company values, but his team ignored them and the effort fizzled out.*

After: *After a recommitment to his company's culture, Scott's team focused on hitting goals while still having fun. They even convinced Scott to shave his head if they reached their goal of $10M in sales. After they hit the goal, Scott cut off his shoulder-length hair and donated it.*

Tactic 1: *Ask your employees what they already value.*

Story: *Instead of writing the values he wanted his company to follow, he asked everyone on his team to write down what makes the company meaningful to them.*

Tactic 2: *Condense the team's responses to core company values.*

Story: *Scott sat down with all the responses he got and looked for common values. Then he picked the ones that he thought would create a fun environment and help his company grow.*

Tactic 3: *Track only metrics that matter.*

Story: *Scott eliminated his customer support team's sales goals because they blocked a core value: "deliver more." As a result, the team started delighting customers. Once, the wife of a customer called to say her husband loved his truck like a mistress, and she wanted to buy a surprise treat for it. After placing her order, the support person sent her a surprise bouquet of flowers with a note that said, "We think the wife deserves a little treat too."*

Tactic 4: *Roll out values one at a time.*

Story: *In the past, Scott posted his company's values and was disappointed that no one lived up to them. His new approach was to roll out each value individually and spend an entire month teaching and reinforcing each one.*

Tactic 5: *Embed each value into the company.*

Story: *At a meeting, he asked everyone to think of ways they could live one of their core values. Everyone wrote down a suggestion. He picked some and got the company to implement them. That's how the company ended up writing cards to customers, sending them free fuzzy dice for their rearview mirrors, and surprising them with gifts.*

Tactic 6: *Recognize and reward employees who live the core values.*

Story: *Scott's team had many prizes made up so employees could give them to coworkers who were living out the company's values.*

27 Interview Structure 3: News

I don't like to focus on the news because its relevance expires fast. When Jon Stewart hosted *The Daily Show*, he was the comic that millions of people turned to when they wanted to understand world events. After he was off the air, his episodes were removed from *The Daily Show*'s website.

Meanwhile, video platforms are outbidding each other for the rights to play reruns of timeless shows like *Seinfeld*.

I prefer to record interviews that will be as useful decades from now as they are the day I publish them. Still, news-based interviews have their place. When controversy strikes, interviews with the person at the center of the storm will draw a large audience. For me, it's also a chance to better understand how entrepreneurs think.

Unlike the Hero's Journey[§25] and how-to[§26] structures, news-based interviews don't follow a clear structure, but they do have common elements. Most interviewers will launch right into the issue that made the news. That's why everyone's there, right? To hold off would be like forcing a thirsty man to listen to a sales pitch before handing him a glass of water.

You can see an ideal example in Oprah Winfrey's interview[14] (transcript[15]) with cyclist Lance Armstrong after news broke about his doping scandal. By then, Armstrong had been stripped of his seven Tour de France titles, lost

---

14. https://www.oprah.com/own/
   lance-armstrong-confesses-to-oprah-video
15. https://www.bbc.com/sport/cycling/21065539

several sponsors—including Nike and Oakley—and stepped down from his Livestrong Foundation.

When he sat down with Oprah, she spent a few seconds explaining there were no ground rules, then got right to the news:

> **Oprah Winfrey:** *Did you ever take banned substances to enhance your cycling performance?*
>
> **Lance Armstrong:** *Yes.*
>
> **Winfrey:** *Was one of those banned substances EPO?*
>
> **Armstrong:** *Yes.*
>
> **Winfrey:** *Did you ever blood dope or use blood transfusions to enhance your cycling performance?*
>
> **Armstrong:** *Yes.*
>
> **Winfrey:** *Did you ever use any other banned substances such as testosterone, cortisone, or Human Growth Hormone?*
>
> **Armstrong:** *Yes.*
>
> **Winfrey:** *In all seven of your Tour de France victories, did you ever take banned substances or blood dope?*
>
> **Armstrong:** *Yes.*

The longer you take to get to the news, the more people wonder if you ever will. The interviewee is also anxious to get to the news and will have a hard time focusing on anything else. So get to it.

When news broke that Stack Exchange, the question and answer platform, was ceasing to allow sites to use its software, I got its founder to do an interview with me. My first question for him: "Joel, you have a bit of news. What's going on?" Many in my audience were going to have parts of their sites shut down because of this decision. They didn't have the patience for me to go through friendly banter.

Once the big news topic is introduced, there are two ways to proceed. The first is to keep pounding away at the news. A classic example of this approach is the 2010 All Things D interview[16] that journalists Kara Swisher and Walt Mossberg did with Facebook founder, Mark Zuckerberg. News had recently come out that Facebook was sharing more personal data than people realized by using a feature called Instant Personalization. In his very first sentence, Mossberg says, "We do have some controversy we have to get through," and starts hitting Zuckerberg with questions about why Facebook makes it so hard for people to protect their privacy.

After 14 minutes of repeated questioning on privacy, Zuckerberg was sweating so much that Swisher suggested he take off his hoodie. They proceeded with another seven minutes of questions on privacy. Then Mossberg announced, "This is my last question on this, seriously." The live audience, exhausted from the barrage of tough questions, clapped when they heard that. Mossberg then addressed the crowd, saying, "I'm sorry if you don't think this is important, but I do." When he finished the privacy questions, he didn't lighten up. Instead, he and Swisher switched to other heavy topics, including questions on

16. https://www.wsj.com/video/
    d8-facebook-ceo-mark-zuckerberg-full-length-video/
    29CC1557-56A9-4484-90B4-539E282F6F9A.html

whether the company had too much power and whether Zuckerberg would continue to lead the company he founded.

Interviews that focus on challenging news from beginning to end are tough to sustain. Guests get uncomfortable and even pugnacious. Audiences feel drained from what feels like non-stop combat. And the interviewer has to endure a verbal battle with someone who's better armed. As Richard Nixon said about his career to David Frost in the most-watched interview of all time, "I know this better than you do. And I should know better because I was there."

The alternative to endless combat is to start with the hard news, then ease off a bit. Give the guest and audience a chance to breathe. A great example of this is the Axios interview with Brian Chesky, the founder of Airbnb. After questioning the company's big decision to go public during the COVID-19 pandemic, Dan Primack asked where Chesky looked forward to vacationing when the pandemic's threat was over. It de-stressed the conversation and gave listeners a chance to get to know Chesky. His answer? He wanted to go to a national park so he could reconnect with the outdoors after the 2020 lockdowns.

I prefer to use the news as a springboard for more evergreen topics that will outlast the news cycle. You can see this approach in my 2009 interview with Alexis Ohanian, co-founder of Reddit. At the time, many experts in the startup community thought Reddit was a copycat of Digg, a more established news aggregator.

My first question: "True or false? You guys saw that Digg was doing well and said, 'Let's jump on that bandwagon.'" I could have spent the hour hitting Alexis with every accusation I read. The live audience watching us online would have been gripped, but that interview would be irrelevant today. Just two years after that conversation, Digg shut down and pivoted, having failed to keep up with Reddit.

Instead of arguing about whether Alexis copied another site, I tried to understand his thought process behind building Reddit in the first place. New entrepreneurs who discover the interview today will still benefit from learning how Alexis decided which business ideas to ditch in favor of focusing on Reddit. One of my favorite parts of the interview was how he talked about Subreddits. Back then, these communities were seen as a failed feature. Even Alexis didn't seem enthusiastic about them. But when he explained how he wanted Reddit to be led and grown by community leaders, he displayed timeless business logic.

So here's my advice to you: conduct news-based interviews because they'll deliver an audience. The top ten most-watched interviews in American history have all been with newsmakers at the center of controversies. But if you want those interviews to have lasting relevance, transition them to topics that endure.

28 Interview Structure 4: Serendipitous

This interview format was popularized by Joe Rogan, the comedian-turned-podcaster who signed a $100M deal to make his show exclusive to Spotify listeners. Rogan can talk to his guests for more than three hours per interview, often with a whiskey in his hand. His conversations bounce between topics like discipline, nutrition, drugs, and exercise, without much more connecting them than Rogan's interest.

These types of interviews seem to lack structure, but when I studied Rogan's transcripts, I saw a clear methodology. I call these interviews "serendipitous" because the host moves quickly through topics, looking for surprise gems. They're like a pub crawler who goes from bar to bar, spending more time in the ones that are fun and moving on the moment things get stale.

A good example is Rogan's interview with Elon Musk, the billionaire behind SpaceX and Tesla. Listen to how fast they zip through topics. They take just seven seconds to greet each other. Then Rogan asks about flamethrowers. Musk gives answers I've heard him give before, so three minutes and 45 seconds later, Rogan ditches the topic.

"Forget about the flamethrower," he says. "How does one decide to fix LA traffic by drilling holes in the ground?" He moved on to Musk's Boring Company, which aims to ease Los Angeles traffic with tunnels.

Five minutes later, Rogan says, "I just don't know how you manage your time," and switches to the topic of productivity. Finally, Rogan hits on a question about artificial intelligence—the opportunities and threats of increasingly intelligent computers. Discovering a topic that's fresh and interesting, Rogan settles into it for 44 minutes.

That's the way these serendipitous interviews work. Topics are disposable. The host moves quickly through multiple subject areas, looking for what's new and fascinating.

How does Rogan keep the conversation about AI interesting for the full 44 minutes? That's longer than a sitcom, and sitcoms have teams of writers. How does he hold people's attention for that long?

The answer is he doesn't. And that's by design, which brings us to the next important element of serendipitous interviews: their purpose.

Alex Blumberg, co-creator of NPR's *Planet Money* and the co-founder of Gimlet Media (acquired by Spotify), has said a big reason people listen to audio shows is companionship. For the serendipitous style of interview, the audience doesn't want their attention held tightly. They're doing other things while listening, like cooking, walking the dog, or exercising. They don't want to focus the way they would during a college lecture or even a sitcom. They want the company of friendly banter while they go about their day.

I don't do serendipitous interviews. I'm too hard-charging for that. I have to have a goal and a process for getting there. Hitting record and hoping for magic would be like asking Michelangelo to throw paint at a wall. That style worked for Jackson Pollock, but Michelangelo was more structured.

Still, I study these interviews to help me improve my style. Once I understood how these interviews worked, I incorporated their approach into my more structured approach. For example, I learned from Rogan that you don't need to exhaust a topic. It's OK to move on to something more interesting.

This more flexible attitude helped me interview David Rubenstein, billionaire founder of the Carlyle Group. I wanted to ask him about how he built his private equity firm, but the combination of finance and politics involved was outside my podcast's focus. I also felt too much resistance from him about going back to discuss a company he was no longer running day-to-day. So I allowed the conversation to keep shifting. We talked about how he prepared for the interview show he hosts on Bloomberg, his firm's use of political influence, his Jewishness, his pledge to give away the majority of his wealth, his leadership book, and so on.

I kept a watchful eye on our mutual interest for each topic and the level of depth in David's answers. When either of those seemed to flag, I allowed myself to move the conversation to another topic.

29 Interview Structure 5: Panel Discussion

Panels tend to be a refuge for the lazy. That's why they're painful for audiences to sit through. It's true of both traditional in-person conferences and emerging online panels, like the social audio pioneered by Clubhouse and video summits done by virtual conferences.

To understand the problem with panels, let's look at a conference I spoke at. As I waited in the green room for my turn on stage, I watched the conference organizer introduce a moderator to his panelists moments before they were to go on stage. The moderator laughed as he told his panelists, "I prefer leading panels to giving presentations because I hate the work of putting slides together." The panelists nodded in agreement. They masked their laziness as a hack, congratulating themselves for getting attention by being on stage, without doing any work.

On stage, the moderator sat limply as he tossed softball questions, like, "Could you tell us about yourself?" Even when they talked for too long or were too self-promotional, he let them go on. Many moderators blame their panelists for not knowing how to give good answers instead of taking responsibility as the leaders of the conversation.

With a bit of effort, you can make your panels engaging and useful. Moderating a panel well is similar to leading an interview. The work is multiplied by the number of panelists you have, but so are the benefits. To do it right and stand out in a crowd of mediocrity, you need to use all the usual tools of a good interviewer. Let's break that down.

Before the event, read every panelist's bio and rewrite it in a way that shows your audience why they should care. Don't let panelists introduce themselves. In my experience, panelists who introduce themselves ramble. Sometimes they ramble because they don't know how to concisely explain what they do to an audience of strangers. Sometimes it's because they want to impress. Sometimes it's because they're just plain nervous in front of a new audience. Take charge from the start by introducing them in a compelling way.

I also recommend talking with each panelist before the day of the event. You don't need to do a formal pre-interview, but ask them about their goals so you can build trust with them by showing you care about their interests. Then ask some of the questions you plan to ask at the event. Since panels tend to be more interesting when there's some controversy, I like to ask panelists for opinions or stories that are likely to shock the audience. Make note of the questions they answer well. Finally, ask them to check the bio you've written for accuracy.

If you can't get on calls with panelists, try to reproduce this work with online research. I was once asked to host a panel at the last minute and didn't have time to talk to the panelists. I gave my producer the list of panelist names and questions I expected to ask. She researched while I flew to the event. When my flight landed, she put together a research doc that was 75% as good as what I would have gotten by talking to the panelists beforehand, which is miles ahead of what other moderators had.

On the day of the event, talk to audience members before the panel starts to learn how to make the conversation valuable to them. At live conferences, I start by walking over to attendees as they wait to get into the venue. I'll explain that I'm leading a panel, and I want to understand what they hope to gain from the event. I continue to ask attendees questions wherever I run into them—in elevators, in lines for coffee, anywhere. For online events, I meet the audience in online groups that the organizers create, on Twitter, or even in the comments of the event's invitation.

I also like to be the first person audience members meet when they walk into the room to watch my panel. I've never seen another moderator do this, but it's a wonderful way to get to know attendees and understand how to make the event meaningful to them. Ask what they want the panelists to answer, what they want to learn, and what they worry won't come out of the panel. Write down both their questions and their names. When you ask a panelist a question and mention the name of the attendee who suggested it, both your audience and the panelists will appreciate that you've done your homework.

For online panels, I like to log into the event early and try to reproduce those conversations with guests. Most online conference software allows moderators to chat with attendees before the event starts. Checking in on the audience's goals and interests helps me calibrate my questions and shows them that my panel will take their needs into account.

When the event starts, before introducing the panelists, introduce the topic. You want the audience to know why they're here. My favorite way to present the talk is by bringing up a problem and explaining how the panel will help to solve it. When I moderated a panel of photographers for an audience of food bloggers, I started by explaining that the audience told me good food photos were the top driver of new readers to their sites, but they struggled to get mouth-watering shots in their kitchens using their camera phones.

Regardless of whether the event is online or off, it's the moderator's responsibility to keep things moving and make sure every panelist has an opportunity to speak. So I gently interrupt panelists who go long, using the techniques I wrote about in the first part[§20] of this book. And I make a mental note of which panelist didn't get enough time to speak, so I can specifically include them.

Most people treat panels as an easy way to get free publicity. Don't fall into that trap. With a little preparation, you can transform your panel into the must-see event of the day.

30 Interview Research

Prep Yourself for Excellence

Once you decide on the structure of an interview, it's time to start researching.

I begin by thinking of all the questions I want to ask my guest. Then I research as many possible answers as I can to give me insight into how they might respond. During the interview, I use the information I gathered to guide my guest and fill in any missing pieces that I couldn't find online.

Many interviewers skip doing research. In fact, some interviewers believe a lack of research is the best way to empathize with the audience. By not doing research, the argument goes, the interviewer can ask the questions the audience would ask if they could talk with the guest.

This isn't just bad advice—it could ruin your reputation with your guest and audience.

I once listened to an interview with Derek Sivers. The interviewer asked Derek what he did with the money he made from the sale of CD Baby, the music sales site he created. By then, it was common knowledge in the startup world that Derek had given the money away. It was part of what made him so captivating. The interviewer had never heard about it.

Your audience doesn't expect you to be like them. They deserve an interviewer who knows more than what they have time to learn. They need you to strive for a deeper understanding than they would reach on their own.

I also interviewed Derek two years before the afore-mentioned interview. I knew from my research that he sold his company for $22M and donated it, so I pushed him for an understanding of how he structured the donation. It turns out he used an estate planning tool called a charitable remainder unitrust, which gave him an income of $1M per year while the rest went into a charitable trust. Now that's something most people don't know about Derek. He found a way to support an organization he believed in while still collecting a million dollars per year for the rest of his life. I was able to help my listeners move past what was known into what was new with just basic preparation.

When I first started interviewing, I did all my own research. Today I have a team that helps me. They put together a research doc to get me started. I add to it myself, but that doc alone does a solid job of prepping me for the interview.

I had never been more thankful for that document than the morning my baby had a diaper explosion. The cleanup took longer than I expected, so I had to rush to the office after. I ended up at my desk seven minutes before my interview started. I didn't have time to research my guest. I didn't know a thing about him. I didn't even know his name. But I wasn't worried. All I had to do was open the research doc, and I was ready. At the end of the interview, my guest asked, "How do you know so much about me?"

Every research doc is broken up into five different sections:

Data: The top of the research doc has links to data—basic facts, not stories. We're living in a world full of data aggregators, and every interviewer should know the tools that relate to their business. Here are some of my favorites:

- **Semrush**[17] tells me which websites send people to my guest's website. It helps me understand a company's marketing.
- **LinkedIn**[18] tells me how many people work at a company.
- **AngelList**[19] and **Crunchbase**[20] tell me who invested in the companies I feature.
- The **Internet Archive**[21] shows me what a website looked like over the years.

Below the data is a timeline of the guest's past experience. Since I'm covering the business side of a guest's life, I like to know where they worked and for how long.

Basic Concepts: I also love having basic concepts condensed into a single sentence. If I'm interviewing a founder about her company, I want a sentence summing up the problem the company solves. If the interview is about a product, I want a sentence describing what it does. If it's about a book, I need a sentence about its purpose. The brevity helps me explain my guest's work to my audience.

---

17. https://www.semrush.com/
18. https://www.linkedin.com/
19. https://www.angellist.com/
20. https://www.crunchbase.com/
21. https://archive.org/

The Hook: The research doc also includes a single sentence hook for the interview. Founders who built a $1M business are everywhere. "How a founder went from homelessness to creating a $1M business" is a story that will get the audience's attention.

Pre-interview Notes: Then comes the most important part: the pre-interview notes. These include summaries of the pivotal stories in a guest's life or the steps they will teach. We already covered the pre-interview notes earlier.§24

Additional Research: The final touch includes excerpts from articles about my guest. If a reporter, blogger, or social media influencer writes something about my guest that might help me, my team adds an excerpt of it to the doc.

You can use outsourcing companies to pull most of this information together. If you provide a clear list of questions, services like FancyHands[22] can put together a decent research doc for about $25. They won't do a formal pre-interview, but they'll do online research to find as many answers to your pre-interview questions as they can. Those services are useful in a pinch, but I prefer to do the research myself or have a team member do it.

Over time we've learned to look for nuances that someone new to interviewing might miss, like inconsistencies in a guest's story. In 2012, I almost interviewed a founder who was building his reputation by implying he was a co-founder of Evite, the online invitation tool. Articles written about Evite in its early days didn't include his name.

---

22. https://www.fancyhands.com/

By discovering that inconsistency, I avoided publishing a misleading interview.

Don't stop researching when your doc is done. My favorite way to research guests is to make phone calls. I have a bad habit of waiting till the last minute to do that, but it's still helpful. In the 30 to 60 minutes before an interview, I text and call people who know my guest—customers, competitors, friends, employees, past interviewees, anyone who comes to mind.

A few minutes before my interview with Rasty Turek, founder of Pex, the video and music database company, I texted a music industry entrepreneur I met in Los Angeles about a decade before.

I promised I wouldn't reveal my source's name, so he gave me as much inside information as he could. He told me that Pex is amazing, but not for the reason its founder was likely to say. He said the founder would probably highlight how the company helps music copyright owners understand how often their music is played online. Sure enough, that's how the company described itself on its homepage.

But the remarkable thing, my source confided in me, was that it helps copyright owners claim their work on YouTube, Instagram, and other platforms. It's controversial because some influencers become livid when their work is flagged or blocked for accidental copyright violations. Still, my source explained, the original creators need a way to claim copyright ownership of their work, and Pex helps them do that. In four minutes, I got more insight than in an hour of online research.

I also asked my source what questions he'd want answered by Rasty. This helped me make the interview useful for a target audience member. It also gave me questions I never would have thought to ask, like how did Pex get away with copying everything on YouTube into its database without getting shut down by YouTube's lawyers?

It can feel uncomfortable calling on your guests' contacts for help. For example, when I called venture capitalist Mark Suster to ask about a founder he knew well and whom I was about to interview, Mark was in the middle of checking into a hotel. It felt incredibly rude to interrupt him. But Mark knew my guest could be hard to get to know based on internet research, so he shared a few personal stories that revealed his personality.

What I realized is that most people want to help interviewers like me. Over the years, every person I've contacted has been impressed that I'd spend the time learning about my guest, even if they preferred not to tell me anything.

Guests respect that kind of research too. When Sam Parr, founder of the media company the Hustle, found out I talked to someone who worked for him, he was impressed and asked, "Do you do this to everyone you interview?" Truthfully, I don't. Every guest is different. But I try to go above and beyond the standard research doc as often as I can.

You don't need to have a producer or pre-interviewer to be prepared. Start by making a list of the questions you most want to ask. Answer as many of them as you can before the interview. If you come across an answer your audience should know, include the question in your research doc anyway. When you get stumped or want more depth, add the question to your outline.

The time you spend preparing will keep your interview unique and valuable. It'll also help you feel more curious and excited about talking with your guest.

31 Personal-Touch Research

Show You Care

Beyond the research that I do to find content for the interview, I also like to do a bit of homework to improve my relationship with the guest.

Attention to detail comes in handy in situations like the pre-interview I did with Gregory Galant, founder of the Shorty Awards (a coveted award for social media stars) and Muck Rack (a tool for helping companies in media.)

The pre-interview with Greg was productive, but he kept leaning back from his webcam for much of it, as if he was trying to protect himself from me. I get it. Doing a good interview is challenging, but *being* interviewed also comes with landmines. Some guests worry they might reveal too much about their companies. Or maybe they'll take credit for something that others did, and their team will think they're self-aggrandizing. Or maybe they think the interviewer has some hidden agenda to bring them down. Whatever their worry, guests can be a bit cagey.

Through my research, I saw that Greg posted about his bike on his personal blog. When I talked to him about it in the pre-interview, he smiled. He went on to tell me about the multi-day bike rides he did. He shared that he carried camping gear on his bike and slept outdoors between strenuous cycling days. And he told me that one of his few splurges after growing his company was buying an expensive bike. He had a big smile on his face as he told me all this. And so did I.

People ease up around non-work and non-family conversations because they are low-consequence topics. If a founder undersells or oversells their startup on my show, it could hurt their business, but if something like bike riding underwhelms or is downright embarrassing, it doesn't matter. It's just a hobby.

Some of the personal-touch research makes it into my interviews, but its primary purpose is to build a better relationship with my guests. A little personal connection leaves a big impression.

You can see an example of the lasting power of that personal connection in a story I heard about Supreme Court Justice Ruth Bader Ginsburg. When she got a letter from five-year-old Naomi Shavin, Ginsburg wrote back and even invited the girl and her family to meet in DC. The offer was very kind, but what struck me about that letter was how Ginsburg noticed the girl was from Georgia and made sure to share that a fellow Georgian, Jimmy Carter, elevated her to the federal bench. She knew Naomi was Jewish and told her that her grandkids called her "Bubby," the Yiddish word for grandmother.

Two decades after that first letter, Naomi still remembered those moments of connection and talked about them in an interview I heard on the Axios podcast shortly after Ginsburg died. That's the power of researching the personal side of people you meet.

Today it's easy to find the personal topics that light people up. Before meeting someone, I often scroll through their Instagram, Twitter, and other social media feeds. I look at the non-work section of their LinkedIn profiles to see if there's something unique about the schools they attended. I Google them and flip past the first two pages to see what stands out. I look for non-work elements of their lives that might be worth talking about.

A great example is when I interviewed Steven Claus-nitzer, founder of Forever Labs, the stem cell company. He posted several photos on Instagram of himself and his kids skateboarding. When I brought it up before our interview, his face lit up. It was one of his favorite non-work activities. I told Steven how worried I was when my wife introduced skateboarding to our kids. His response was so insightful that I included it in the interview:

"Skateboarding is the perfect thing for kids to get into if you want them to have resilience and just be goal-oriented. In order to ollie on a skateboard, you've got to try hundreds of times and fall. It's going to hurt. You're going to have to get up if you really want it. You'll keep going, though. And eventually, you're going to ollie, right? It's a perfect metaphor for life in general. If you're going to be successful in life, you're going to fall a bunch of times."

In a science-heavy interview, talking about kids and skateboarding was refreshingly relatable. And it showed Steven that I cared about him as a person, not just his business. All I had to do was scroll through his Instagram feed.

Take the time to do personal research. It's worth it.

32 Self-interest

Put Your Needs Upfront

Many people sit behind a mic and think they've suddenly turned into the reporters they see on the evening news. They think the professional thing to do is get the facts for some imagined audience that expects formality.

That's the old way. It doesn't work online, where you don't have a general audience. Your audience is made of enthusiasts who want to learn about their passion from someone who is just as passionate as they are. They want to know about you as much as they want to get to know the person you're interviewing.

I miss this point myself sometimes. When it was time to hire someone to help me lead my company, my business coach told me to interview Cameron Herold, the former COO of 1-800-GOT-JUNK, the junk removal service. "I can't," I told her. "Mixergy is about interviews with proven founders who talk about how they built their businesses. He didn't found 1-800-GOT-JUNK."

Like a good coach, she kept pushing. "You're dealing with a challenge every entrepreneur in your audience will face at some point. Ask him."

I finally listened to her. When I published the interview, I titled it, "Cameron Herold Coaches Me on Hiring (So I Don't Collapse at My Desk)." We talked about how I budgeted money to buy and mail a microphone to every interviewee, but I didn't have time to coordinate it. And how I sometimes read about founders who listened to my interviews and had successfully sold their companies, but I didn't have time to reach out to them to do interviews with me. As Cameron coached me through delegating, I learned from him, and so did my listeners.

It became the most listened-to interview of the year, with double the average audience of the year's other interviews. Even founders who didn't need the advice told me they liked hearing what was going on in my life. They had listened for years and felt invested in my success—or were at least curious about it.

Audiences today don't mind when you put your needs first, as long as they align with their own needs. Still, it's difficult to do in a society that punishes self-interest.

Even if you haven't read Dale Carnegie's book, *How to Win Friends and Influence People*, when it comes to human relations, you're living in a world it defined. Since 1936, when it was published, it's consistently been one of the best-selling self-improvement books. But something is missing from the book's philosophy.

Its message can be summed up as follows: if you want people to like and listen to you, you need to take an interest in them. It's sensible. By taking an interest in people, I didn't just make friends, I got my ideal after-school job, working for someone who has stayed a lifelong friend.

But there's a problem with exclusively taking an interest in others as a way to build relationships. I discovered this lesson in college while on the subway home from school. A classmate mentioned he liked comic books, so I asked about them. He went on and on about his collection. As he talked, his eyes lit up with excitement. He loved the conversation and liked me for tapping into his passion, but it was torture for me. I have no interest in comics.

I remember wondering, "Is this what being a good conversationalist is all about? Sacrificing my enjoyment just so someone else would be happy and like me?"

Long before I started interviewing, I experimented in conversations. After that interaction on the subway, I decided I would no longer sacrifice myself. It became clear that showing a little self-interest during a conversation was good for me and my relationships. No one wants to hog speaking time if the other person isn't genuinely interested.

Years later, I was invited to a party in LA by a venture capitalist. One of the guests loved talking my ear off about his company. The more interested I was in what he was saying, the more he loved talking to me. Truthfully, though, I wasn't interested. Eventually, I decided to cut him off with that magical phrase described in Part I:

"I'm sorry to interrupt," I said, "but you mentioned earlier that you live in Los Angeles. My fiancée and I are getting married here. What do you think about raising a family in LA?"

He said, "It's a wonderful city, but painful when you have kids."

I saw he had an emotional connection to the topic—a topic I was also interested in—so I continued, "Painful? Why?"

"Andrew, my kids know about things that they shouldn't."

Now he was getting personal, so I pressed on, "What's going on with your kids?"

He could see my genuine interest and wanted to help. "We have a nice car, but my seven-year-old son knows about expensive car models that no kid his age should know about. And he expects us to buy them. We have a maid, but his friends have *full-time, live-in* maids. He wants to know what's wrong with us that we don't because he's embarrassed."

As we talked, I could see he appreciated talking about an issue he'd been thinking about deeply, and he enjoyed helping me with a problem that I was sorting out. Before I left, he gave me his cell phone number, so we could continue the conversation if I ever needed to.

Soon after that, Olivia and I got married ... and moved to Argentina.

That's the kind of meaningful conversation you want to have, especially on a podcast.

When COVID-19 hit the U.S., I went to a grocery store to stock up on food because of reports of upcoming shortages. As shoppers cleared the store shelves to prepare for an uncertain future, I saw the fear and anxiety on their faces. I became worried about my business, my family, my health, everything. I needed to avoid feeling pessimistic, so I used my interviews to help me.

I put out requests online for introductions to entrepreneurs who found ways to do well in those difficult times. That led me to interview people like Aditya Nagrath, whose Elephant Learning app was used to teach kids math at home during school shutdowns. He showed me that parents were taking a more active role in their kids' education, and there was an opportunity for entrepreneurs to help.

I also interviewed Sahil Lavingia, whose Gumroad platform allowed creators to sell their work online. He told me how creators who previously procrastinated about selling digital products were finally becoming entrepreneurial.

As I heard what was working for entrepreneurs, my pessimism about the future dissipated. I saw an opportunity to build my company to serve the new needs. Many of my audience members noticed the same opportunity. Those interviews were such a hit that I temporarily changed the subtitle of my podcast from "Mixergy" to "Recession-Proof Startups."

As an interviewer, you have an opportunity to reach people who can help you with your biggest challenges. Don't shy away from using that power. When you follow your self-interest, your interviews will find an audience with similar needs, and you'll be the person who finally helps them overcome.

33   Audience Intel

Uncover Their Needs

It can be valuable to put your needs front and center during a conversation. But that doesn't mean you ignore your audience. Audience intel is one of the best ways to steer your interviews toward the most painful and productive lessons.

My favorite form of audience intel is Scotch Night, which came up in the section about the dramatic lowball technique.[§11] I've hosted these events for years. The premise is simple: I'll buy three different bottles of Scotch (along with snacks and other beverages) and invite people to my office to try them. As you might have guessed, this event really isn't about the Scotch—it's about having time to get to know people who listen to my interviews. In this casual and intimate atmosphere, folks share things they would never think to include in an audience research survey.

During one Scotch Night, an entrepreneur in attendance started the evening talking about the early success of his new business. He sold flashing car rims—a surprisingly lucrative industry. He hit over $100K in annual sales within months of launching. That was a big win for him.

But as the evening went on, and he became more comfortable, he shared how anxious he really was. "How do I know when I should quit my full-time job and focus on this business?" he asked.

I never would have thought of that problem. After graduating from college, I jumped right into entrepreneurship. I never had a full-time job while nurturing a side hustle. And at first glance, reaching six figures in sales seemed like the right time to quit a job. But as we talked, he explained how unpredictable car rim buyers could be and why he didn't want to give up the security of a good job.

He asked me: "Would you ask your guests how they knew it was time to leave [their full-time jobs]?"

I said I would, and I did. What I learned from those interviews was useful to the many new side-hustle entrepreneurs in my audience.

Oprah Winfrey, despite her fame, also knew the power of one-on-one audience intel. Winfrey always signed autographs after her live shows, but in the early years, she would try to get through them as quickly as she could.

"I [would] do all the autographs and never look up, trying to get through 350," she said. "One day I decided, 'I don't want to do that anymore.' But what do I really want to do? I want to talk to this audience. I want to find out who they are, where they come from. That became my favorite part of the day."

So Winfrey started talking with members of her live audience after each show. It helped her understand them—why they spent hundreds of dollars and hours of their time to see her. She considered it her greatest resource. "It's the reason why we were number one for 25 years," she said.

You don't have to drink Scotch or be Oprah Winfrey to learn more about your audience. Another one of my favorite tactics is to offer free, one-on-one coaching calls. People thank me for helping them, but they're helping me too. By bringing me their problems, they're guiding me toward interview topics that will be most valuable to other *Mixergy* listeners.

Here's the best part about coaching calls—as an interviewer, you don't have to solve their problems. Your job is to find guests to address those challenges. You should also be a good listener, which is what most people want—someone to let them talk about their problems and find their own solutions.

If those options don't jive with you, there's a simpler way to get started with audience intel: be like Barbara Walters. I know it's not fair to ask you to be like one of the greatest interviewers of all time. But Walters had a surprisingly simple strategy for developing interview questions.

I studied Walters to see how she made the Shah of Iran's wife cry, how she persuaded the elusive Fidel Castro to spend hours talking with her, and how she got Richard Nixon to admit he should have burned the evidence that cost him his presidency. In these historic interviews, when the camera panned back to Walters, I could see a set of notes in her lap—her questions. She wrote them over and over again ahead of time, but she didn't do it alone.

In her autobiography, Walters explained her process. "I wrote down on three-by-five cards as many questions as I could think of, then asked anyone who walked into the office, whether it was somebody delivering the mail, a production assistant, or a hairdresser, 'If you could ask any question of [whomever], what would it be?' It was very productive."

Asking people what questions *they* would ask your guest is the simplest form of audience intel. Today you see interviewers do this on social media, which has the added benefit of helping them promote the upcoming interview. They'll post, "I'm going to interview [whomever]. What questions should I ask them?" The responses can be helpful because it uncovers people's curiosity about the guest.

This approach has its limitations. When the guest isn't well-known, audience questions tend to be superficial. As I mentioned in Part I, I don't have many superstar guests on my show, so I rarely ask my audience what questions to ask. I prefer to ask them about the topic they know most about: their own problems. Then I use my interviews to address those problems.

Regardless of how you do it, the important thing is to uncover your audience's needs and curiosity. And when their interests align with your own, you're in for a fantastic conversation.

34 Get Back to Purpose

Overcome Any Problem

A few years back, I decided to try something brand new.

I was going to conduct in-person interviews … in Estonia. It would be part of my larger goal of running a marathon and conducting an interview on every continent.

My hosts in Estonia were LIFT99, a community of successful tech startup founders, who invited me to record in their office. As I set up, my mind flooded with the worries of a rookie. I had ten years of interviewing experience by then, but the wildly unfamiliar environment had me nervous. I was recording in person, using new and unfamiliar equipment. What if my microphones and recorder failed? What if I didn't know enough about the people I was interviewing? What if they regretted giving up time with their families to record with me on the weekend?

Sitting in the conference room they lent me for the day, I tried to think of anything other than my nerves. If I didn't, I was sure to make a mistake setting up my new equipment or fall back on excessively flattering questions in an effort to be liked. I thought back to my first interviews to remember how I handled anxiety back then. What got me through the early days was focusing on my higher purpose.

I started Mixergy after a massive failure. I poured $300K of my own money into an online invitation site that was so bad that my wife would not even use it. After the company went under, interviewing became my way to learn how other founders built their companies. I wanted to figure out how I could do it better next time. I wanted to remember what was fun about entrepreneurship. And I wanted to provide all that to other entrepreneurs.

Those first recordings were horrendous. I didn't know how to use an equalizer, so fans had to lower the volume to hear me stammer through questions and raise it when my guests responded. But I didn't let those mistakes stop me because I needed my guests' insights. I was desperate. I was on a mission.

Years later, when I asked fans why they listened despite the audio issues, they said they needed those answers too. They were on similar missions.

So that's what I did in Estonia. I reminded myself what brought me there. It all started when I looked for an old note on my computer and discovered a list of ten-year goals instead. I felt like a failure when I read it. Ten years were nearly up, and I hadn't achieved any of them. Even though I misplaced the list, those unmet goals lived somewhere in the back of my mind, haunting me.

I was in Estonia because I decided to start with the goal that excited me most: run a marathon on every continent. I also decided to interview founders on every continent about how they reached their goals. Then I'd find a way to do the rest of the things on the list.

So when I was nervous or worried about the equipment, I shifted my focus to my mission: achieve my ten-year goals.

My trip paid off when I interviewed Ahti Heinla, the Estonian co-creator of Skype. He told me how Skype was built and sold to eBay for $2.6B. Focusing on the weight of my unaccomplished goals, I kept my nerves in check. I asked him how he reached his next goal. He saw how important this conversation was to me and confessed he didn't hit it.

"Everybody who was early at Skype, and founded another startup after Skype, failed," he said. "It was a hard landing for everybody."

I could imagine how tough it was. My failure to hit my ten-year goals was private. His failure was public.

My equipment worries disappeared as I asked what he did next. He told me he stopped trying to build a mega-successful startup. He was going to have a daughter and so decided to take a break. As a hobby, he built robots and entered them in robot battles. That's when a thought occurred to him. His robots were getting so sophisticated—what if they could be used to deliver food? He launched a new startup, Starship Technologies. Soon colleges signed up to use them for food deliveries on campus. The startup grew. By not trying so hard, Ahti achieved more.

The next day, I sat with my iPad in what felt like an old Soviet coffee shop, and I went through my list of goals again. I realized I didn't really care about most of them. One of the biggest items on the list was to grow my online invitation site. I had closed that business years ago. Interviewing became my business, and I loved it so much more than running that invitation site. So I decided to liberate myself from the demands of that list. I was free to enjoy life and pursue new interests.

To get to that realization, I had to tune out everything else and focus on my mission.

It's not just inner chatter that you need to tune out—audience expectations and ratings can distract you from your mission as well. The hosts of the *All-In* podcast learned this lesson the hard way when they covered the Robinhood vs. Gamestop debacle in early 2021.

The show is hosted by four famous investors who talk about tech, startups, politics, and life. They pride themselves on giving no-BS takes on the biggest issues of the day. When Robinhood, the stock-trading app, halted trades of Gamestop during a massive short-squeeze, the internet erupted with outrage. This was the type of newsworthy story that the *All-In* pod feasted on. The hosts landed an interview with Robinhood's founder, Vlad Tenev, to feed the audience's appetite.

The result? The *All-In* pod momentarily became the most popular tech podcast in the U.S. and 11th overall on Apple Podcasts. But it nearly destroyed the show in the process.

The hosts felt like they couldn't be harsh with Tenev because their audience expected them to support entrepreneurs. At the same time, they couldn't go easy on him for shutting down trading because their audience also expected them to hold leaders accountable. The result was a lukewarm interview that neither pushed Tenev nor satisfied the audience.

Co-host Jason Calacanis said fans of the show "barbecued" them. Another host, David Friedberg, thought the pandering interview was so bad that he threatened to quit. As co-host Chamath Palihapitiya said in a postmortem, "We got caught up a little too much in ratings: 'Where is it ranking?' 'How can we go higher?' And it's that gamification of people's reactions that caused us to do that."

Whether you're worried, nervous, or just excited, the way to center yourself as an interviewer is to focus on the mission. What is your higher purpose? For me, that mission is to learn how to be a better entrepreneur and let my audience learn along with me. What is yours?

35 Ditch the Outline

When You Must Wing It

Everyone has a plan until you get punched in the mouth.

Mike Tyson's famous insight applies to interviews as much as it does to boxing.

You should go into every interview with an outline. That's why I gave you five different interview structures to work from. But if you aren't willing to ditch your plan, you'll miss opportunities and cause unnecessary friction with your guests.

I've learned this lesson the hard way—on multiple occasions. The first time was when I interviewed Fred Wilson, an investor and Twitter board member. The week of our interview, Fred found himself at the center of a controversy between Twitter and startups building apps for its platform. Business Insider reported:[23] "Holy Cow Did Twitter's Top Investor Drop a Bombshell on Twitter App-Makers Today." Fred seemed to say that Twitter was going to put those small companies out of business by stealing their best features.

But instead of bringing up this news during our interview, I rigidly stuck with my original outline. I focused on how he built his venture capital firms and made early investments in fast-growing startups like Etsy, Twitter, and Kickstarter. In hindsight, I missed a massive opportunity to report on something newsworthy *and* educational for my audience.

---

23. https://www.businessinsider.com/
holy-cow-did-fred-wilson-drop-a-bombshell-on-twitter-app-makers-today-2010-4

Another time I stuck with my plan too tightly was at my first live event in front of three hundred fans. I interviewed three entrepreneurial giants on stage: Gary Vaynerchuk, Tim Ferriss, and Hosea Jan "Ze" Frank. By the end of the event, all three of them were frustrated with me.

My goal was to understand how they built their businesses by creating passionate fans. When Gary handed out sweatbands featuring his wine show's logo, I grilled him on how he came up with that cool-looking swag. He kept telling me he didn't know how his creative process worked. He definitely didn't use the step-by-step approach I was pushing him to articulate. Regardless, I questioned him relentlessly because we had agreed that I would dissect how he built his business. I was obtuse.

The mistakes kept piling up. Since my interviews usually lasted an hour, I kept firing off questions, even though people at a live event don't sit still for long. Attendees started talking to the bartenders and each other, but I didn't let up. The panel went way longer than it should have, all because I had an outline, and I refused to accept the need to set it aside.

After my live event mistake, I accepted that I had to toss my preparation aside when I sensed a better approach. That became harder when I started working with producers who pre-interviewed guests. I hated ignoring the notes my producer worked so hard on, especially since I knew my interviewee also dedicated time to the pre-interview call. But both my guests and producers were grateful when I set aside my outline because I felt there was a better conversation to be had without it.

My on-stage interview with Gary, Tim, and Ze needed a major detour from the outline, but most instances are less dramatic. The more common experience is when a guest insists on telling a story in a way that's less interesting than an experienced storyteller would tell it. I have to accept that. It's their story, not mine. As an interviewer, you can't bully your guest into telling their story your way. If you must reshape their story's structure, do it in editing (but be faithful to their intent), not in the conversation.

The outline—and every other interview tool—is in service of a good interview. If you think there's a better conversation to be had without those tools, set them aside.

36 The Billboard

Grab Attention Fast

Movie producers use billboards to get people into theaters to watch their films. Few podcasts have the luxury of that kind of budget. Instead, listeners use the first few seconds of each episode to decide whether or not it's worth their time.

Just how important is your opening? Reality set in for many podcasters when Anchor, the podcast creation app, gave its creators second-by-second analytics for each episode. When podcasters looked at their graphs, many saw big drop-offs in listenership just moments after their podcasts started. Some lost over half their listeners within a minute. As NPR producer Nick Fountain said, "If you don't hook people in within the first minute, you're screwed."

This isn't just true for podcasters. The principle applies to nearly every medium. In our attention-starved world, the first few seconds of any content are the most important.

Interviewers don't have traditional billboards, but we still need creative ways to capture and keep our audience's interest. Here are four billboard techniques you can use.

Billboard #1: The Why

The easiest way to introduce an interview is by telling listeners why you chose the interviewee and why you think it's important for them to listen. I used this opening with

Tara Reed, founder of Apps Without Code, which teaches entrepreneurs to build software without programming.

I introduced her by saying that I spent years rejecting listener suggestions for me to interview her. Frankly, I didn't believe good apps could be built without code. But then I tried no-code tools for myself and realized how big the possibilities were. Later I discovered that Tara had raised money from Silicon Valley investors for a software company built entirely without code. Finally, I decided I *had* to interview her. I had a responsibility to help non-developers in my audience understand this new way of building software companies.

Billboard #2: The Shocking Question

Another way to hook listeners is to begin with a shocking question. One of my favorite opening questions is to ask founders how much revenue their businesses generate. That signals to my audience we're going to get into topics that are usually considered too personal to discuss in public.

Oprah Winfrey used this technique in her interview with cyclist Lance Armstrong. Her first question to him was, "Did you ever take banned substances to enhance your cycling performance?" Does an interview get any more captivating than that?

But remember my advice[§15] from Part I: if you're worried about a guest's response to your shocking question, pre-ask it before recording. Make sure they're prepared to answer and continue with the interview. You don't want them so caught off guard that they shut down for the rest of the conversation.

Billboard #3: The Rule of Three

Sometimes, one hook isn't enough. NPR producers like using the **rule of three**,[24] a principle that says focusing on a trio of events makes the material more enjoyable and memorable.

When podcaster and founder of AppSumo, Noah Kagan, interviewed NPR producer Nick Fountain, Noah illustrated this principle. At the start of the episode, he recorded a summary of the top three lessons from the interview. He said, "I learned three major things that I'm going to share with you today. Number one, how to hook your listeners. Number two, why editing is king. And number three, how to create a real narrative for your work and closing out what you make."

Billboard #4: The Cold Open

A fourth option is to clip a highlight from the interview and play it for the audience before the interview starts. LinkedIn founder Reid Hoffman often uses this technique on his show, *Masters of Scale*.

In his interview with Richard Branson, founder of Virgin Group, Reid pulled a clip in which Branson talked about heading to a party at Las Vegas's towering Palms Hotel. Upon arriving, Branson was surprised to learn he would be entering the party by jumping from the top of the building! The story is certainly interesting in itself, and it showed listeners that this wasn't just another business interview.

---

24. https://en.wikipedia.org/wiki/Rule_of_three_(writing)

Whether you choose one of these four suggestions or take another approach, the important thing to remember is this:

> *At the start of your interview, your listener is not asking, "What does this interviewer have in store for me?" but "Do I really want to listen to this interview?"*

PART III: LANDING GREAT GUESTS

Now that you know how to prepare and carry on meaning-ful conversations, it's time to talk about your guests. This section will walk you through how to find the right people to interview.

37 Superstars: Why You Don't Need Them

Before writing this chapter, I looked at my download stats for the year. Who was my most popular guest?

I expected it to be the founder of Riot Games, creators of the worldwide sensation League of Legends. Around 115M people played the game in 2020. More people watched the League of Legends World Championship in 2019 than watched the Super Bowl. Clearly, he has a following. He was a sharp guest with a compelling story. But no, his interview didn't get me the year's biggest audience.

The title of most popular *Mixergy* interview for 2020 goes to a founder whose company is significantly less known. Andrew Burnett-Thompson is a quiet developer who built SciChart, software that allows other developers to add helpful charts to their apps. Why was his episode so popular?

Andrew had good jobs working for big companies like energy giant BP. But he was fascinated by the entrepreneurs he heard on my podcast and in the startup world. He decided to teach himself to code by reading programming books and doing one lesson per day. Then, when he realized how hard it was for developers like him to create charts, he decided to launch a company to solve the problem. He got up early every morning and worked while his wife and baby slept. On his train ride to and from work, while others fiddled with their phones, he pulled out his laptop and coded the foundation of his startup's software.

When his company finally broke the $1M revenue mark, he tweeted about it. A few people in the startup community congratulated and retweeted him. Several pointed out his accomplishment to me and thought he was the model for how they wanted to create a company. So I invited him on. His story was even more compelling when we got into the details.

As far as I can see, I was the first person to interview him. Meanwhile, a Google search for interviews with the founder of Riot Games leads to 660,000 results, including interviews with *VentureBeat*, GameCrate, and *The Founder Hour*.

And there's the difference. The founder who was lesser known was someone my audience could relate to. He had already generated buzz in the entrepreneurship community by tweeting and blogging about his experience. But no one else had interviewed him. I had a monopoly on the Andrew Burnett-Thompson story.

That pattern has been true every year since I started.

Podcasters seem to want the most recognizable guests. I do too. Landing a superstar is like a stamp of approval for your show. It elevates your reputation as an interviewer. Still, I've found that lesser-known interviewees can drive bigger audiences, and they're significantly easier to land.

The key is to find people whom you know your audience will relate to. They need to see themselves in your guest. Look for niche communities where your audience hangs out. Following my listeners and their heroes on Twitter helped me land Andrew, but there are loads of other places.

When I started interviewing, some of my top guests were obscure entrepreneurs like Drew Houston and Brian Chesky. They were popular in a tiny online community called Hacker News,[25] the online meeting place for developers who built startups. It's grown a lot, and so have its members. Drew's Dropbox and Brian's Airbnb went on to become massive entrepreneurial success stories. At the time I interviewed them, they were only famous in the small startup world.

Reddit has a small community called Entrepreneur Ride Along,[26] where founders post updates on their new businesses for other entrepreneurs to "ride along" and learn. Rohan Gilkes was a regular contributor, sharing how he was modernizing cleaning services with a site he created, Maids in Black. His updates were getting a lot of attention. I thought he had an interesting story, and the popularity of his posts told me that other entrepreneurs did too. So I invited him on. He was one of my most popular guests, and his interview continues to bring in new listeners—people who either want to see how he started his company or learn how they could take another industry like his into the online world.

Your go-to communities will change over time. When I started, Hacker News was my favorite place to find guests that people cared about. Later it was Product Hunt,[27] where tech and startup enthusiasts vote on new products. Most recently, Indie Hackers has become my best resource.[28] Entrepreneurs use it to share their startups, including revenue, and other entrepreneurs comment and vote on these stories.

---

25. https://news.ycombinator.com/

26. https://www.reddit.com/r/EntrepreneurRideAlong/

27. https://www.producthunt.com/

28. https://www.indiehackers.com/

A good way to find communities of potential guests is to use traffic analysis tools like Semrush[29] and Similar-Web.[30] Enter a website into their search bars, and they can provide a list of communities that the site's audience visits.

A better way to find potential guests is to talk with your listeners and ask where they hang out online. They'll help you find communities that traffic tools can't, like private chat groups. They'll also help you identify nuances no traffic tool can communicate, like their level of passion for the community.

When you find communities full of ideal listeners, join them. They'll signal to you who they want to hear from.

---

29. https://www.semrush.com/
30. https://www.similarweb.com/

38 Superstars: How to Land Them

I strongly believe that you don't need superstar guests. Less than 10% of the interviews I've done have been with big-name people. It hasn't stopped me from building a solid personal brand, a large audience, and a strong business from my interviews.

Still, landing the occasional big shot is worth the work because they'll help grow your audience and increase your credibility with other interviewees you're trying to land.

The challenge is that celebrity guests who are in demand usually don't have enough incentive to sit for an interview with you, or even respond to your request. There are times, however, when they're eager to be interviewed. I call those times **motivated moments**.

A motivated moment is when a popular author is releasing a new book and wants to try to hit the bestseller list. It's when a reclusive movie star suddenly appears on multiple talk shows to promote a new TV series, or a billionaire founder is launching a new startup and appears on podcasts he's never heard of before.

The best way to spot motivated moments is by browsing lists of upcoming releases. Most industries have them. Amazon lists upcoming books by topic and release date. Techmeme has stories about startups that just raised money. IMDb lists upcoming movies. Part of every interviewer's job is to watch these sites and find out what's coming up. That's how I land marquee guests.

When I did a live event in my former hometown of San Francisco, I needed a guest who'd be such a strong draw that people would fly from other parts of the world to hear their interview. A motivated moment helped me find that person.

Tim Ferriss was about to release a TV show. *The 4-Hour Workweek* is the most cited book by successful entrepreneurs I've interviewed, but Ferriss can be a hard guest to land because he obsesses over minimizing distractions. Still, the upcoming launch of a new show can use as much attention as possible.

We emailed. He said yes immediately. He showed up to the event and was a huge hit both with the in-person audience and listeners who heard the recording on my podcast. He also helped grow my audience. He tweeted the interview to the over one million people who follow him on Twitter, and some of them subscribed to my podcast.

His appearance was amplified by his fans. Celebrities like Tim have dozens of fan sites and social media accounts. They tell fellow fans what their hero is up to. Several of them mentioned our interview, which helped me grow my audience.

A motivated moment helped me book billionaire founder of the Carlyle Group, David Rubenstein, soon after he published his book, *How to Lead*. It also helped me book one of Silicon Valley's most successful entrepreneurs and investors, Justin Kan, soon after he launched Exec, the assistant service. And after Steve Huffman, co-founder of Reddit, launched a travel-booking site Hipmunk, I asked to interview him about it. I used the interview to also talk about the massively successful Reddit. That interview was a huge hit on Reddit, which helped me draw a big audience.

Motivated moments make booking guests easy—sometimes a little too easy. You might have noticed that your favorite, elusive author suddenly appears on every TV show, YouTube video, and podcast after publishing a book.

They say yes to so many outlets that you find yourself getting bored of hearing their stories. If you go after big shots during their motivated moments, it's important to be early to interview them—ideally, be the first.

The other thing to keep in mind is that a motivated moment closes fast. After working hard to promote a project, most people want a break from talking about it. I noticed that's especially true of authors. When I asked a prolific author why that happens, he told me there's a huge gap between expectations and reality for books. When a writer sees how few people read books and how little impact they often have, their disappointment can be so big that they can't stand to talk about it.

So when you find a motivated moment, move fast.

39 Newsmakers

Build Your Audience and Relevance

The most-watched interviews in mainstream press have always been news-based. In 1993, when Michael Jackson was accused of child sexual abuse, he sat for an interview with Oprah Winfrey. It became the most-watched interview in American history, with 90M people tuning in. The Top 10 list of most-watched interviews is full of politicians, royalty, and accused criminals who made headlines around the world.

But you don't need to land worldwide headliners to take advantage of breaking news. All you need are people making headlines in your audience's world. My world is the tech startup community. One day, two well-known people in my world became newsmakers.

I read somewhere that Matt Mullenweg was upset. As the founder of WordPress, the world's most popular web-publishing platform, startup founders paid attention to what he said. Matt was frustrated that Chris Pearson, a popular designer and software engineer, had the audacity to sell a WordPress template instead of making it free like the WordPress platform itself.

Bloggers in the WordPress community were writing about the fight. So were large tech news sites. Meanwhile, people on both sides of the argument were tweeting their opinions. It was big news in the startup world. So I asked both Chris and Matt if they'd let me interview them together via Skype to understand each of their points of view. They agreed.

After I published it, hundreds of sites linked to the interview. For years afterward, people in the WordPress community made sure to tell me what they thought of the debate and whose side they were on. That's the power of news-based interviews.

The way to land newsmaker guests is to pay attention to the news in your world and quickly send invitations to the people at the center of the stories. At first, it seems hard to get people who are in the news to agree to an interview. The world is talking about them. They must be too busy. But what I've found is that these busy news cycles are just another motivated moment. The people in the news are often as eager to clarify their stories as listeners are to hear them.

The key is to jump on the news as fast as possible. If the person you're after says they're busy and asks to do it a few days later, tell them that in two days they won't reach as many people. Let them know that people make up their minds fast and change them reluctantly. If they don't give their side of the story, the world will have solidified their opinion of them without their input. They need to capitalize on the story while it's hot if they want to reach as many people as possible.

⬦ CAUTION A word of caution: don't destroy relationships by being desperate for a story. You want to maintain good, long-term relationships with your guests, so don't pressure people to do interviews that aren't in their best interest.

When I first asked Gagan Biyani for an interview, he turned me down. He was the founder of Sprig, a food delivery startup that raised over $50M in funding before shutting down. I kept checking in with him, and he kept insisting he wasn't ready to talk about it. Three years after the shutdown, he agreed to let me be the first person to publish an interview about the story. Be patient.

But if there's a chance to land a newsmaker, don't waste time. And don't assume that if your reach is too small, newsmakers won't want to be interviewed by you. I used to think that way, then I turned my disadvantage into an asset. I started telling people at the center of controversies that my smaller audience would mitigate their risk. If they flubbed their story on CNN, the world would know. If they did it on my podcast back when it was unknown, the impact would be much smaller. This is one case where a smaller audience can help you.

Another thing to help you land newsmakers is your mission—your higher purpose. In a world full of "gotcha journalism," practice "I get you journalism" instead.

People in the public eye are surrounded by "gotcha journalists" who try to make a name for themselves by extracting scandalous revelations. That's not my goal or the aim of this book. We want to say to our guests, "I get you. I understand who you are and want to learn more." Most high-profile guests appreciate that. It can be disconcerting to have their lives dissected and evaluated by people who've never met them. They want an honest chance to give their perspective.

The trickier part of landing these guests is getting through to them, although it's easier than it used to be. Social media platforms like Twitter and Instagram make it simple to send private, direct messages. Whois domain searches help me find phone numbers of website owners. Sales prospecting tools like Hunter.io[31] and RocketReach[32] allow me to find practically anyone's email address.

---

31. https://hunter.io/
32. https://rocketreach.co/

If you're tech-savvy, you'll find new opportunities for connections constantly. For example, I discovered that if the person I want to reach has an iPhone, I can easily reach them by text. All I need is their email address, which is easy to find. If I pop that into Apple's Messages app and send a text, it'll show up on the recipient's screen instantly. Using FaceTime, I can use their email to make an audio-only call that comes across like any other phone call.

As clever as all those methods are, my favorite way to reach guests is to ask for a referral. Everyone I interview becomes another helpful connection in my personal network. The interview booking software I use, Acuity Scheduling,[33] automatically adds all their contact information to my phone's address, so I have multiple ways to reach them. If I need to reach a newsmaker or anyone else in a hurry, I can text or call past guests and ask for introductions.

---

33. https://acuityscheduling.com/

40 Role Model

Land Guests with the Help of Their Heroes

It can be hard to persuade guests to do interviews. So I call on stories of their heroes to help me like I did the time I wanted to interview a writer who was at the center of a scandal.

I used to check TechCrunch the first thing after waking up. I wanted to see what was new in the startup world that I loved. One Friday morning, I woke up and read that a TechCrunch writer, Daniel Brusilovsky, "allegedly asked for a Macbook Air in exchange for a post about a startup."

I emailed Daniel about doing an interview. He told me he was a big fan but couldn't do it. The news just broke. It was too soon.

I could understand the embarrassment of being called out by the tech press, including *VentureBeat, Gawker, Silicon Valley Watcher*, and *Huffington Post*. I wanted to reassure him that he shouldn't view this scandal as a reputation killer—that sharing his side of the story in an interview could actually help him.

Daniel was a startup junkie like me. He respected entrepreneurs who took risks and bounced back from failures. Instead of pleading with him to do the interview, I emailed him this:

> *The entrepreneurs you admire have done some crazy stuff in the past. Here's a line from Richard Branson's Wikipedia.*

> *"In 1971, Branson was arrested and charged for selling records in Virgin stores that had been declared export stock."*

A few minutes later, he agreed to a phone call. Then he agreed to do an interview with me.

Stories like Branson's arrest are iconic—almost startup folklore at this point. The more common stories I share come from guests I previously interviewed. If a founder raised money from Y Combinator, I might tell them about how the founders of Y Combinator did my podcast, and I'll mention a few other startups who raised money from them. If a potential guest is an investor, I might reference my past guest David Rubenstein, founder of the Carlyle Group.

Referencing the heroes of your potential guest is a powerful form of social proof. But when I first started *Mixergy*, I didn't have enough well-known guests on my show. People I interviewed, like Zappos founder Tony Hsieh, were successful but not yet well known. I needed to find a way to get interviews with instantly recognizable people.

Conference organizers know that industry celebrities draw large crowds. Those speakers were the type of heroes that would be perfect for helping me recruit interviewees.

I decided to go to startup conferences and seek out these well-known speakers. I would attend their keynotes and wait for them to get off stage. Then I'd ask them, "Can I interview you right now?" After grabbing their attention (and typically overwhelming them), I would dial back my request and say I just wanted to ask a few quick questions. They still weren't enthused to do it, but asking a couple of questions seemed reasonable compared to an entire interview, so many of them agreed. This is how I got interviews with Tim Ferriss, influential blogger Brian Clark, and Apple co-founder Steve Wozniak.

These recordings didn't set the world on fire. Tim's lasted only 39 seconds, and Steve's consisted of him telling a joke about Steve Jobs. Still, these short interviews gave me social proof and allowed me to show off my interviewing skills. In some ways, the short clips worked better because potential guests just wanted a quick understanding of who I was.

When I reach out to founders I want to interview, I usually send just a three-line message. For many years, this was my pitch:

> *Can I interview you on Monday at 9:00 a.m., Pacific about how you built your business?*
> *This is for Mixergy.com, where I interview founders about how they built their businesses.*
> *You can see a sample of my style in these short interviews with Tim Ferriss (link), Brian Clark (link), and Steve Wozniak (link).*

Over time, as I landed higher-profile guests on my main show, I replaced these short interviews with lengthier ones.

People want to emulate their role models and heroes. You can use this desire to land interview guests. But if you're low on potential guests to contact, you need to start thinking like a salesperson. That's next.§41

41 Salesperson's Technique

Get Referrals

A couple of years after launching my interview series, I started running out of guests to interview. My network of entrepreneurs was sizable, but it wasn't infinite. How could I reach outside my network but still get quality guests?

Many of the entrepreneurs I interviewed had a similar problem, like Naomi Simson, founder of RedBalloon, which enables people to gift experiences, such as hot air balloon rides and car race days. When she ran out of contacts at companies that offered experiences, she asked her suppliers for referrals. That did the trick.

Since many businesses use referrals, I figured interviewers could too. And I found a way to make them even more powerful.

If you listen to my early interviews, you'll hear me ask guests for referrals within the interviews ... with my whole audience listening. I wanted to share my approach with my audience and show them how I was thinking about upcoming guests. It also had the benefit of committing my guests to follow through on their offers to introduce me.

This is how I met one of my best interviewees. When I interviewed Tikhon Bernstam about how he built Scribd, the document-sharing site with over 100M monthly users, I asked him, "Who do you know that I should be interviewing the way I just interviewed you?"

It used to be that when I got a referral for an interview, I would say, "Thank you. Could you introduce me?" Top salespeople I interviewed taught me to say instead,

"Thank you. Who else?" and keep growing my list. As it happened, I knew and interviewed the first people Tikhon thought of, but then he mentioned someone I hadn't heard of before: Emmett Shear, the co-founder of Twitch. Emmett had helped Tikhon with how to grow his business.

"Can I hit you up for an introduction to Emmett?" I asked him, with my recording going, so my audience could hear the interaction. "Absolutely, anytime," he said. A few days later, I interviewed Emmett, who told me about the process he went through to build Twitch, the video broadcasting site that he ended up selling to Amazon for $970M in cash.

And how did I meet Tikhon? The previous month I interviewed David Rusenko about how he built the website builder Weebly and quietly got over 11M websites to use it. I asked him for an intro to founders he respected most. Tikhon was at the top of his list.

Keep asking good interviewees for people like them. If you're interviewing people within a small niche, this technique could be the best way to find new guests. If you're in a space where people tend not to respond to strangers, this could be your *only* way of getting guests. There's nothing more effective than a trusted friend saying, "I think you should do this interview. I did it too."

And if you're in an expanding industry like the one I focus on—tech startups—there's simply no way to know everyone worth talking to. You need people in the space to tell you who's there. I could probably supply my podcast with a new guest every day for the rest of my life with this one technique alone.

The only downside of asking for referrals is the lack of variety. People tend to refer other people similar to them. Tikhon, Emmet, and David are all male entrepreneurs who raised capital to build their startups and were in the Y

Combinator accelerator program. To attract a diverse set of guests, you must be very intentional. Explicitly ask for referrals to people from different backgrounds (such as bootstrapped founders) or underrepresented groups. Use this technique to break into new social circles and expand into those worlds.

If referrals aren't helping you find enough interview guests, or the right kinds of guests, add this next technique[§42] to your system.

42 Idea Fountains

Develop Ongoing Sources

Bob Hiler was tired of hearing me talk about my struggle to find strong interview guests. Every week we'd get on a coaching call to talk about what I was working on, and every week I'd talk in circles, grasping for ways to find my next guest.

"This isn't working," my coach said in frustration. "You can't keep looking for ideas. You need idea fountains."

I immediately Googled to see what it meant.

"It's not in Google," he said. "I just made it up. On each call with me, you look for one guest. What if instead of looking for one new guest each week, you search for one *source* of new guests? Try it now. What do your most recent best guests have in common?"

I looked at my list and said, "They each sold a company."

"Perfect," Bob said. "So your new idea fountain is to search for the latest companies to be acquired and invite the founders to do an interview."

"That's no good," I shot back. "Days after an acquisition, founders often can't talk publicly. The company that acquired them wants to manage the story. But if I search for companies acquired three months ago, that would be pretty easy."

"Excellent!" Bob cheered me on. "Now you have your first idea fountain: companies that were acquired three months ago. Do this search for yourself first to see if you like the results. Then pass it on to your assistant to manage, and we'll move on to finding more idea fountains."

Together Bob and I found other idea fountains, each of which provided a steady stream of new interview guests. We discovered that authors of upcoming books were eager to do interviews and had thoughtful things to teach, so Amazon's upcoming book section became an idea fountain.

We realized that listeners shared my interests and often met people who'd be perfect for me to interview. So we added a "Suggest an Interviewee" link to my site's homepage. Anyone can use the link to connect me with an interviewee to consider. This became our best idea fountain.

Some idea fountains ended up leading to less-than-spectacular results. For example, I tried pursuing founders who were recently on other reputable podcasts. I thought the screening process for those shows would vet guests for me. I also assumed the guests would be better storytellers since they'd been on other shows.

In fact, the opposite was true. Having told their story before, guests sounded too scripted or kept mentioning that they'd already told the story on another podcast. I hated hearing a guest respond to one of my questions with, "As I told Courtland on Indie Hackers ..." So I dropped that idea fountain.

The important lesson I learned from Bob was to stop looking for guests individually and instead look for sources of guests—**idea fountains**.

I also applied idea fountains to other areas of my business. Searching for good advertisers is a constant challenge for a podcast like mine. Instead of thinking of individual companies, I started looking for idea fountains. I put a "Sponsor My Podcast" link on the site, and it became a major source of new advertisers. Emailing my audience was another source of sponsors. I made a list of the products I paid for to run my business—if I'm already a customer of those companies, they're more likely to become sponsors.

Idea fountains have also helped me create better in-person events. When I travel to conferences, I host dinners to get to know other attendees and find potential podcast guests. Finding dinner guests one at a time became a time suck that turned dinners into distractions. So I looked for idea fountains. One was conference speakers. If the organizers thought enough of someone to invite them to speak at the conference, I'd want to meet them, so I invited them to my dinners. Another idea fountain was the Contact Plus app. It simplifies finding friends in cities I travel to by adding location data to my online contacts.

Stop searching for one guest or one idea at a time. Instead, look for *sources* of people and ideas. When you find your idea fountains, you'll develop a strong pipeline for every part of your business.

43 Fans, Assemble

Ask Your Audience To Help You

The startup community was enthralled by Fred Wilson. As a social media pioneer, he was an early user and investor in some of the world's most popular apps: Twitter, Kickstarter, Etsy, and other companies that reshaped the internet and our communities.

My audience wanted to hear from him, and I wanted to interview him. But he wasn't replying to my emails. I'm not sure he even saw them.

So I did something I had never done before—I asked my audience for help. I made a public plea for someone to connect me with Fred. I asked my fans during live streams. I blogged about what I wanted to learn from him. I told my email subscribers how badly I wanted this interview.

And then, something amazing happened: my audience came through.

One of my listeners happened to work in the same building as Fred. He used my call to action as an excuse to strike up a conversation with the notoriously cagey investor. That got things started. Then a few listeners found Fred's email address and sent him requests. Another nudge. Other people sent him private messages on platforms I'd never heard of before. Each little bit helped.

Finally, Mike Colella, a longtime *Mixergy* listener and founder of ad research company AdBeat, happened to see Fred teach at the Future of Web Apps conference. Mike asked Fred for an interview on my behalf. This time Fred said yes. Mike introduced us by email, and I finally got my interview. The interview became one of my most popular of the year, and it gave me credibility with companies that aspired to build the next Twitters and Kickstarters of the world. They wanted to hear how the person who backed those companies thinks.

But my public cry for help did more than just connect me to Fred. It tightened the bond between me and my listeners. We were a team, working against the odds to land a big-time guest. They were part of creating the interview with me. Mike and I went on to be friends for over ten years, and he was one of the first people to visit my house when I moved to San Francisco. He later became a *Mixergy* guest when Adbeat took off.

Here's the most amazing part: my audience continued to help me find new guests, some who weren't even on my radar. When Foursquare launched, it became the most talked-about startup in the tech world. The word was that its founder, Dennis Crowley, turned down "generational wealth" from a company that wanted to acquire it. He became one of the most sought-after founders in the country for everything from jobs to investments to interviews. I didn't even try to jump in the fray. I figured I'd come back and get his story when things died down.

But then, out of the blue, AppSumo founder Noah Kagan emailed me an intro to Dennis. Noah was a friend and *Mixergy* fan and knew I was always looking for good guests. After talking with Dennis, Noah sent an email encouraging him to do an interview with me. All it took was a reply from me to book an interview with one of the hottest founders of the year.

My podcast now gets an average of 11 inbound interview requests every day, but I still ask my audience for introductions. They often connect me to people and trends I'd never find myself.

I needed my audience's help more than ever in 2019 when I decided to do in-person interviews (and run a marathon) on all seven continents in a single year. I couldn't figure out which countries to visit, let alone find and vet potential guests in places where I didn't speak the language. So I turned to my fans. And again, they came through.

I wasn't sure where to go in Latin America, so Nathan Lustig, who invests in startups there, got on calls with me to help me understand what's working there and whom I should meet. I planned to go to a big country in Europe, but Ragnar Sass, who founded the sales platform Pipedrive, opened my eyes to how his home country of Estonia was producing more startups per capita than just about any part of the world. And in South Africa, Adii Pienaar, founder of WooCommerce, which turns websites into online stores, invited my wife and me to his house and introduced me to entrepreneurs with whom he had spent his professional life building relationships.

The hardest place on Earth for me to reach on my tight schedule was Antarctica. Because of international agreements, environmental concerns, and harsh conditions, there are limited flights to Antarctica. But Eric Miller, a listener and adventurer, knew an organization that supported expeditions to Antarctica. He helped me catch a flight on an old Soviet plane so I could complete my goal.

It takes time to build trust with your listeners. But ironically, asking for help actually creates *more* trust with your audience, not less. Don't be afraid to reach out to your network and make a public plea. You never know who might show up to your aid.

44 Say No

Turn Them Down Without Offense

When you're just starting out as an interviewer, it's hard to get guests. When you're established, it's hard to turn down guests. But if you say "yes" to every request because you're too scared to say no, your quality will inevitably dip. And your audience will notice.

As tough as it is, you have to learn to turn down interview requests. I'll show you the right way to say no and help you avoid the wrong ways.

For years I turned people down the wrong way. I once got on a call with a prospective guest because a mutual friend asked me to consider him. He was a nice guy, but I quickly knew I didn't want to interview him. His company was too new. He hadn't done much yet. And frankly, I just wasn't curious enough about him. So I told him, "I'm sorry, but your company is too new. I can't do this interview, but I'd love to have you on when your company grows a bit."

I thought I was clear, and we'd just move on. He didn't want to. "As a listener, I can tell you that you need to feature more new companies," he said.

I should have known he wouldn't back off. People in promotion mode tend to be persistent. If they're not, their startups could die. So he kept pushing. The more I explained myself to him, the more I could feel him digging in his heels. This went on for several minutes. It was exhausting for both of us.

Here's a key lesson I've learned from the entrepreneurs I've interviewed: if a problem comes up multiple times, you need to systemize a solution. So I started hunting for a solution to my problem of saying no to unqualified guests. That's when it hit me.

In Part I, you learned how to communicate difficult information by putting the words in someone else's mouth.[§14] This same technique can be used to say no. The next time an unqualified guest asked to be interviewed, I told them, "I admire what you have planned for your company, but when I interview founders of smaller companies, my audience complains and sends me angry emails. It's not worth it for you and me to get that kind of treatment."

That solved it. And it's the truth. Whenever I interview founders who don't fit the mold—whether they're too small, too big, or not founders at all—my fans let me have it. They honestly have higher standards than me.

Occasionally, I'll be sheepish about using the technique, like the time I talked with a public relations rep of a venture capital firm that wanted to be on my podcast. The firm was so helpful to me over the years that I didn't want to give her a systemized answer, so I explained all the reasons the interview wasn't right for me. She offered a counter argument for each of my reasons.

Finally, I said, "In recent years my audience has complained when I feature investors instead of entrepreneurs."

She said, "My client wouldn't want that. Let's not push it."

Sometimes, you want to tell your guest why you're turning them down and give them a chance to correct your information. I've turned down founders whose businesses didn't seem big enough, only to be proven comically wrong when they show me their financial dashboards via screen share. But when it's time to say no, depersonalize it. Put the rejection in someone else's mouth. Tell them who, other than you, would have a problem with the interview and why.

If you don't have a big, vocal audience to blame when you're turning down a guest, look for someone else. Did you promise your sponsor you'd focus on a certain type of guest? Say so. Does the interview fall outside of your commitment to your boss or someone else? Say it.

If there's no one else to point to, blame your higher purpose and guidelines. Even this will depersonalize the rejection and take some of the sting out of it. What you need is an outside force that will eliminate resentment and end arguments.

PART IV: THE BUSINESS OF INTERVIEWING

I intentionally focused this book on the timeless craft of interviewing and not the business of interviewing. I wanted the ideas to be as true in the future, when conversations might be held in virtual reality, as they were when I did a one-on-one interview in a cold tent in Antarctica.

But many readers are interested in how to turn interviewing into a marketing channel, a side hustle, or even a full-time career. If that's you, certain business fundamentals are necessary to master if you want your interviews to be sustainable over the long term.

45 Guest Promotion

Reaching Their Followers

Promotional techniques change constantly and are best left to marketers to teach. But there's one approach that's unique to interviewing and vital to mention: get help from your guests to promote your interviews.

Guest promotion can be varied and unpredictable. When I interviewed Paul Graham about how he launched Y Combinator, one of Silicon Valley's most prestigious startup incubators, his firm featured my episode on their homepage for months. Vishen Lakhiani, founder of Mindvalley, the online education company, used Facebook ads to promote his interview and drove traffic to my site. But most guests don't do anything to promote their interviews with me.

What a guest does with an interview after it's published is out of the interviewer's hands. However, there are ways to nudge them toward helping you promote their episode.

I learned the most powerful technique from a friend who runs an interview podcast that's often on Apple's Top 10 list. Before the interview starts, he lists all the ways he'll promote his interviewee. He'll share it in his email newsletter, post it on his popular Instagram account, and so on. He'll spread his guest's message far and wide. Then he turns to his guest and asks, "How can you help me promote you?"

In the moments before an interview starts, the guest is at their most vulnerable. They're worried about the questions they'll be asked and how they'll do. In other words, they want to be liked. They'll promise to do things like share the interview with their email list and on social media. And once they've promised, they'll feel obligated to live up to their commitments.

I tried this technique. It was incredibly powerful, but I quickly ditched it. It framed the interview as a promotion piece for the guest, so they didn't want me to ask tough questions and often asked me to edit out potentially embarrassing stories.

I interview because I want to understand how people think, not be part of their self-promotion machine. So I stopped asking guests for promotion help right before the interview. I'll always choose substantive conversations over downloads.

Still, this technique reminded me of the power of simply asking, so I found a way to do it that felt good. My assistant, Andrea Schumann, was already emailing guests when their interviews were published. I asked her to add a small request to those emails. She simply asks guests to promote the interviews if they want to.

The results weren't as dramatic as when I put guests on the spot before my interviews started, but it helped. When I put guests on the spot right before their interview, about 75% agreed to help promote. Now, when Andrea asks after the interview is published, we get about a 15% promotion rate. You'll have to decide what's best for you, but I prefer this approach because it prevents guests from treating me like a marketing channel.

What's worked better for me is looking for promotion beyond my guests. Many interviewees are connected to people who have an incentive to promote them. A good example of this is Quin Hoxie, founder of Swiftype, a search engine that tens of thousands of sites use to allow their readers to search their content. Quin had a tiny social media presence, so asking him to promote the episode wouldn't have led to many listeners.

But one of his investors was Alexis Ohanian, co-founder of Reddit and Silicon Valley icon. Alexis had an incentive to promote the company he invested in, so he shared the interview on Twitter. It gave me exposure to Alexis's massive following and added to my credibility in the tech startup space.

It also taught me a new way to promote interviews organically. Instead of simply relying on guests, find their supporters and ask them to promote the interview. For example, ask an interviewee's investors to post on social media or private message the company's social media accounts and ask them to share. A founder might not want to say "look at my interview" on social media, but their head of marketing might want to post "look at our amazing leader."

Other supporters with incentives to promote include the following:

- Publishers, following an interview with their authors.
- Mentors, when guests mention them in their interviews.
- Friends of the guest with big followings who want to support them.
- Other companies—like software tools—that guests say they use and love.

All it takes is a short message along the lines of, "I interviewed the founder of a company you invested in. If you think your followers want to hear it, here's a link for you to post."

Or, "I interviewed Claire, and she told me your software helped grow her business. I'd love to get more people to hear her story. If you think it'll help your followers understand how good your software is, please share my interview."

As with anything else you want in life, if you want your guests to promote your interviews, you must ask for it. And don't limit your request to your guest. Think creatively about the people who have a vested interest in promoting your work.

46   The Booking System

Organize Your Business

My interview booking process used to be a mess, and it took up too much of my time.

I never knew if my pipeline of upcoming guests was big enough or if I had to scramble to find new ones. I had to approve or reject every single guest myself. My producers didn't know whom they needed to pre-interview. When they got on calls with upcoming guests, they didn't know what the interview would be about. All this uncertainty meant I often got 6:00 a.m. text messages asking for solutions to problems that could derail an upcoming interview or damage my relationship with an upcoming guest.

At the time, my wife was just a few months away from giving birth to our first child. I realized I couldn't be both a good dad and a good interviewer unless I solved the chaos.

So again, I tapped into what I learned from my successful interview guests and created a system for managing interviews. The system allows my team to do their jobs well without needing my help, and it gives me the freedom to focus on doing meaningful interviews.

I use Pipedrive,[34] a customer relationship management (CRM) platform. I picked it because it's goal-oriented and process-driven. The first thing you need to do when you start using Pipedrive is decide on a goal for each contact. For us, the goal is a published interview. Then you have to lay out each step toward that goal. Our team has ten clearly defined steps, which I'll describe in this section. Once you do that, Pipedrive allows every member of your team to collaborate and shepherd contacts through each step.

Regardless of what tool you use, find something that clearly defines the steps you need to publish an interview. Your tool also needs to be collaborative so that multiple people can move guests through the process.

In Pipedrive, each step of the booking process has its own column. Each potential interviewee is assigned a contact card that starts in the first column. The card moves along each column until their interview is published. We change up our steps as needed, and if we have a problem, we add a step to address it. If a step becomes unnecessary, we eliminate it.

---

34. https://www.pipedrive.com/

As of mid-2021, these are our steps, along with an explanation of each one:

1. **Suggest Guest:** Anyone can add a potential guest to this list. People who work at Mixergy log right into Pipedrive and add anyone they want. Those outside the company (listeners, PR people, entrepreneurs who want to be interviewed, etc.) use the suggestion form on Mixergy.com. When a form is submitted, a contact card is automatically created and added to this column in Pipedrive.

   Regardless of who adds a guest to this list, we want as much information as possible to help us contact the guest and decide if they're a good fit for our audience. So, in addition to name and company name, we ask for a suggested interview topic, growth metrics, and articles that help us learn about the potential guest.

2. **Approve Guest:** Using the information we collect in step one and the vision for the type of guests we're looking to interview, a producer decides whether to move the guest to the next step in our process.

   When we reject guests, we sometimes write a note about why they're not a good fit, so future team members learn how we make decisions. Nobody is ever deleted from the CMS. A guest who isn't a good fit one year could be perfect in the future when their company grows, or if they launch something new.

3. **Find Contact Information:** Finding a way to reach out to a potential guest used to be a difficult process of asking friends in the industry to help, but it's much easier today. Sites like Hunter.io allow us to find email addresses for almost everyone we'd want to interview. If that fails, we can usually reach people through a direct message on social media.

If all that fails, we can reach out to past intervie-wees who might know the guest I want to interview.

4. **Invite to Do Pre-interview:** Once we find a prospect's contact information, we email them a request to have a conversation with our producer. That's when their card moves to this column in our software.

5. **Remind to Do Pre-interview:** I added this step when I looked at why we lost so many prospective guests. The benefit of using sales software is that it shows us at what stage in our process we lose people. Turns out, only 25% of people who were invited to do an interview bothered to respond to our email.

   So I tested sending a follow-up email. That helped increase our numbers beyond 50%. Now, if a guest doesn't respond to our interview request within a week, we send a second email instead of removing them from our booking process.

6. **Book Pre-interview:** As soon as a guest adds them-selves to our producer's calendar, we add them to this stage in our booking process. At this stage, the pro-ducer has clear guidance about what the interview will cover. Each suggested guest's card in our software has their company name, growth metrics (revenue, num-ber of customers, etc.), a suggested interview title ("How a Homeless Man Founded a Multimillion-Dollar Software Company," for example), and maybe even a few articles.

   Our producer can change the interview's headline, topic, and anything else she wants based on her own research or conversation with the guest. But she never has to text me at 6:00 a.m. on the day of an interview and ask, "Who is this person, and why am I talking to him?"

7. **Did Pre-interview:** After the producer pre-interviews a guest, she moves their card to this column.

8. **Remind to Book Interview:** Guests who've been pre-interviewed know that their next step is to book an interview. They usually do it on the call with our producer. But, sometimes, they procrastinate. They may tell our producer they need to consult someone before scheduling and then forget to do it.

   So we added a step to remind them that they did all the hard work. Now all they have to do is schedule an interview with me and enjoy the conversation.

9. **Booked Interview:** When a guest books an interview, my assistant adds them to this column.

10. **Done:** When I finish recording an interview, my assistant moves their card to this column.

Mixergy episodes are hardly edited before publishing. This is by design. I love the sound of a raw conversation. But I know this style isn't for everyone. If you choose to edit your episodes, add an "Editing" column to your system before the "Done" column.

When an interview is finished, we mark it as "Won." That's a sales term, as in "we won the sale," but it feels appropriate for interviews. We did all the work to find, prep, and interview. The interview is live on our site and all the major podcast apps. Pipedrive even throws virtual confetti to help us celebrate the win. We won.

And the right booking system will help you win, too, without the headaches.

47 Sponsor Revenue

Develop an Income Stream

It took me a year of publishing three episodes a week to finally feel "ready" to sell ads on *Mixergy*. The truth is, I had no idea what I was doing. But step-by-step, I built a sponsorship revenue stream that took my little podcast from a hobby to a full-time business with multiple employees.

In this section, I'll share my story of how I landed my first podcast sponsor, scaled ad revenue from less than $50K to over $400K in three years, and created a system that makes money with minimal effort.

Some podcasts will be ready to sell ads faster than I was. Some slower. No matter what, your podcast sponsorship journey will go through three stages: startup, growth, and maturity.

The Startup Stage

The startup phase began a year after I started interviewing and felt ready to look for my first sponsor. At the time, I didn't know what to charge. I didn't even know how many people listened to my podcast because the publishing software I used didn't keep track of listenership.

The startup stage of sponsorship sales is full of unknowns for both creator and sponsor. That's why you should start with learning, not selling. Then, when you start selling, prioritize getting data from sponsors over making money from them. And, to eliminate the uncertainty for them, guarantee results.

I first needed to answer a simple question: How much could I charge? There's no ad platform for podcasts that will automatically tell you the value of your show. I had to find someone with some experience who would be friendly enough to help me. Scouring online message boards, I met Sunir Shah, an ads buyer from FreshBooks. At the time, FreshBooks bought a lot of advertising on podcasts similar to mine, so I asked Sunir if he'd help me understand ad sales. I sent him a link to all the interviews I had recorded to show I was serious. He and the FreshBooks team gave me invaluable advice. They taught me how they bought ads, which sites performed well for them, and what great ads looked like.

New content creators and publishers are intimidated by ad buyers. I've found it helps to remember that it's an ad buyers' job to find new, productive places to advertise. They want to work with us.

After talking to FreshBooks, I realized my interview podcast could get them customers, so I pitched them. I suggested a low price of $750. At that rate, they told me they needed 40 new customers to try their invoicing software. That information was more important to me than getting paid. If my ads generated only 20 users, I would know to charge $375 in the future. If they generated 80, I'd charge future sponsors $1,500. In the ad startup stage, it's hard to know what your ads are worth without data from your sponsors.

FreshBooks was hesitant at first, even at that low price. I understood. They tried ads with other new publishers, and some didn't work. Mine could be duds too. So I guaranteed my results. If I didn't get them the number of customers they needed, they wouldn't have to pay. I was fine giving a refund. The important thing to me was knowing the effectiveness of my ads.

I was so eager for numbers that I came up with a way to double-check their work. When I recorded the FreshBooks ads, I told my audience that if they signed up, they should send me a test invoice. Since my audience loves inside information about business, I said that if they invoiced me, I'd hit reply and tell them how much FreshBooks paid for the ads. The invoices started hitting my inbox immediately after I published their first ad.

Within days of the first ad run, FreshBooks told me they hit 38 users and that they expected more to trickle in. My ads really were worth $750. I started selling ad space to other sponsors at that price. I explained that FreshBooks tested them, and they worked. Once you get one well-known customer, it's easier to get others to at least test you. By asking sponsors for metrics on the ad's performance, I could gauge the best time to increase my rates.

Growth Stage

The startup stage was defined by selling single-episode ads to individual sponsors. My goal during that stage was to acquire data, not make money. With data in hand, I felt confident to move to the next stage of ad sales: revenue growth.

I hired Sachit Gupta, a business development consultant, who helped me realize that my reputation was strong enough for companies to invest in long-term relationships with my audience. Before I started working with Sachit, my sponsors were companies with relatively low-cost products. They needed to acquire a lot of new customers to make the ads worthwhile.

To increase my ad rates, Sachit suggested going after businesses with high customer lifetime values (LTV). That meant they only needed a few new customers to be profitable, and they'd be willing to spend more to acquire them.

A good example of a high LTV sponsor is Toptal, which helps businesses hire top developers and other professionals. Though prices start low, it's not uncommon for a Toptal client to spend tens of thousands of dollars per year on developers. Customers don't make that kind of decision after just one ad. It took time and repeated exposure to Toptal ads. Sachit realized that based on my reputation, Toptal would be willing to invest in a long relationship and multiple ads.

He was right. His insight took our sponsorship revenue from under $50K annually to over $200K within a year. He doubled it the following year and kept growing it by working with sponsors that earned more from their customers by establishing longer relationships with them.

Maturity Stage

The maturity stage of the ads journey can be traced back to a little link that's been on my site for over a decade. It simply says "Sponsor." It links to a form where businesses that want to sponsor my interviews can tell my team about themselves and schedule a call to talk about buying ads.

Today, every single show sponsor uses that link to start their relationship with me. Ad buyers find it because of the reputation my site built over the years. Each interview I publish draws in new listeners. Some of those happen to be ad buyers who want to buy podcast ads. Each link to my site adds to my reputation with Google, which helps me show up higher in search results done by ad buyers. Each new article written about my work is another potential source of sponsors.

My job isn't to hunt for new sponsors anymore. It's to talk to each potential sponsor and make sure that what they have to offer would be a good fit for my audience.

48 Sell to Your Audience

Solve Their Problems

I'm surprised by how many interviewers will pitch socks, mattresses, and other random goods for their sponsors but never sell their own products to their audiences.

You might be OK forgoing the revenue, but by not selling your own products, you're missing an even bigger opportunity: to understand your customers and make their lives better in ways that only *you* are qualified to do.

Pat Flynn is a master at selling products to his audience that solve real problems. Pat has been interviewing about as long as I have. One of his favorite topics is the art of podcasting. By talking to podcasters in his audience, he realized that one of their biggest frustrations was posting their podcasts on their own websites. That's because traditionally, podcasts were meant to be played in dedicated podcast apps. With this insight, Pat created Fusebox, an audio player you embed on your website. He nailed a problem that plagued my business for years. I've been a grateful customer of Fusebox for a long time.

There's a satisfaction that comes from solving your audience's problem in a way that no one has before. But you don't have to build a software product. Jamie Masters sells coaching. Jason Calacanis sells access to his angel fund. Sam Parr sells research.

The important thing is to understand your audience well enough to know their pain. To do that, many marketers recommend sending surveys. I hate filling out surveys, so I rarely send them out. I also don't like how survey responses tend to lack depth and details.

My preference is to offer coaching calls. When people talk with a coach, they tend to open up about their issues because they need help. They offer deeper insights than a survey could ever elicit because the conversation allows the coach to ask probing questions.

Several years back, I decided to diversify my income beyond ad sales. I could sense that some of my listeners were struggling with something, but I couldn't figure out what it was. Some sent me complicated mind maps that they made based on what they learned from their favorite entrepreneurs. Others asked me if I could create a search engine to find and listen to specific parts of my past interviews with entrepreneurs.

So I put out a call for listeners who needed coaching. I left it vague because I didn't want my preconceptions to limit what they asked for. I simply said I'd help listeners with their business issues. Then I got on Skype with them to talk. Most of what they asked for I couldn't help with. That's fine. As an interviewer, you don't have to solve every problem. If I couldn't help, I said I'd ask future interviewees about the issue raised.

Eventually, the coaching calls helped me find a pattern. Listeners liked my interviews because they heard *what* was possible in entrepreneurship. But they struggled to figure out *how* to execute on those opportunities. That's why they made mind maps and wanted detailed search options. They were trying to decipher the steps to accomplish what my guests had accomplished.

Developing a solution for my audience took a lot of trial and error, but it eventually became my favorite revenue source because it addressed a real need. Instead of helping listeners hunt through my interviews for the how-to content, I invited the entrepreneurs I interviewed to teach master classes.

These master classes are essentially how-to interviews with clear visuals. If you read the section on how-to interviews, you understand their structure. I sell them on a subscription basis. For only $399 a year, listeners get access to all my master classes.

Over 200 entrepreneurs have taught master classes so far. A few examples: Sam Parr, founder of the Hustle, taught the step-by-step process he used to get his first 100K email subscribers. Ankur Nagpal, founder of Teachable, the software used by over 100K teachers, taught how to create and sell a profitable course based on data from his most successful users. And Justin Kan, who founded Twitch, the live-streaming site that was sold to Amazon, taught how to create products people want.

Master classes seem like an obvious solution in retrospect, but I had to try several different approaches before settling on this. I tried Action Guides, which were written based on interview transcripts, but they lacked depth. I tried live webinars, but listeners outside the U.S. couldn't show up because of timezone issues. I tried selling recordings of individual master classes, but I couldn't get enough viewers to make the instructors happy. At each step, I talked with my customers, understood their problems, and tried alternatives.

My in-depth conversations with the audience and the resulting understanding of their needs are what make product creation one of my favorite parts of the interview business.

49 Not Giving Up

How to Create Momentum and Keep Going

I've talked to dozens of people who started podcasts and quit after just a few episodes. Many were embarrassed—they had good conversation skills but could only produce a handful of interviews. What was wrong with them?

I feel for them. In fact, I was in their shoes. Episode #8 of *Mixergy* was almost my last.

Episode #8 was with Bill Reichert, founder of Garage Technology Ventures. I remember thinking how hesitant he seemed to talk with me. My interview style was completely unpolished. Our conversation was full of "ums" and "ahs" and slow responses. I worried he regretted interviewing with me because my audience was so small.

Afterward, I felt like such a failure that I wanted to give up interviewing. I was ready to quit. But I couldn't. Not because I was determined—my motivation was all but gone. I couldn't give up because I had already scheduled more interviews.

A friend of mine had already introduced me to Tyler Suchman, a search engine optimization expert, which was a new skill at the time. And I had already booked Tara Hunt, who was teaching people, like the founder of Zappos, about social media. I had to keep going because I'd already committed to interviewing them and others.

The best way to ensure you keep going is to schedule interviews ahead of time. Most new interviewers do the opposite. They schedule a few to get a sense of the format and then plan to schedule more after evaluating the first batch. This is a mistake because your first episodes will almost definitely fail to live up to your expectations. What you need is momentum. We live in a self-help world, where we're taught that people become successful through intrinsic motivation. That's not the only way to get ahead. Let your commitment to another person drive you—or rather, *pull* you—even when you doubt yourself.

In the more than ten years I've been interviewing, I've rarely had a month without at least five guests booked in advance. That's how I keep getting past my inner doubt and continue improving.

Inner doubt is powerful. It can stop us. But it's also a liar. Years later, I went back to read a transcript of my interview with Bill. I realized it wasn't nearly as bad as I thought at the time. With the benefit of a decade of experience, what I perceived was his discomfort was actually an expression of vulnerability. In the interview, he admitted to investing in about 100 internet startups at the worst time in the industry's history: the Dot Com crash. Instead of feigning invincibility, Bill admitted to a mistake. It was the beginning of the type of openness that built my show's reputation. Good thing I had interviews scheduled after that and didn't give up.

When I moved from California to Argentina, I had no idea what my new home country would be like. Where would I record? Would the internet be stable? Would our remote locale cause a lag and screw up my conversation's rhythm? There were so many challenges. But they didn't stop me. Before I got on my flight, I scheduled interviews for just a few days later. That forced Olivia and me to race through Buenos Aires looking for an office to rent. I remember the pressure. But it also allowed us to explore different parts of the city. Most importantly, it strengthened my commitment to the interviews.

And it all worked out. I found a good office. I had a strong internet connection. I recorded my interviews.

You'll always have challenges and doubts about your work. I still do. The 2,052nd interview I published was with Ray J, the musician and tv star. I wanted to understand how his earphones company, RAYCON, did over $100M in sales. For an hour after it was done, I didn't want to talk to anyone because I kept going over in my head all the things I could have done differently. Was I too complimentary? Did I drive hard enough for numbers when he told me he struggled financially at times? Should I have done *this*? Did I do too much of *that*? I felt lousy.

Doesn't matter. It didn't stop me because I had four interviews scheduled for the following week and four more for the week after that. I created momentum to keep myself going.

When Ray J's interview was published, listeners told me how much they loved it. They didn't know all the questions I wished I had asked or things I wished I had done differently. The interview had much more substance than my inner doubts allowed me to realize.

The only way to keep going is to have more interviews scheduled. Keep your calendar full.

PART V: FINAL WORDS

50 Using What I Taught You

This isn't a book of rules. It's a book of tools.

My goal isn't to bind you to what worked for me but to give you ways to enjoy interviews and learn from them.

I started writing this book at a challenging time. San Francisco, my hometown of nine years, went into lockdown to prevent the spread of the COVID-19 virus. I went from working at an office I loved to recording my interviews on a small card table in a corner of my bedroom. I was miserable about the change and didn't fail to mention it in interviews.

I started writing this book to do something meaningful in my newfound solitary time at home. It was my chance to help interviewers.

As I wrote down my hard-earned lessons from over a decade of interviewing, I rediscovered each of them. The techniques that have become second nature through years of use became more useful as I remembered why they worked. The ones that I forgot about reentered my interviews.

Reconnecting with the craft of interviewing made each interview I recorded from the corner of my bedroom more fun. In the hour that I recorded with each guest, it didn't matter where I was physically because I was vicariously experiencing life through my guests' stories.

I missed having a drink in person with friends while our city was in lockdown, but in many ways, the hour I spent in an interview was better. Only experienced interviewers know how true that is. Regular conversations are full of small talk, fillers, and distractions. In an interview, you can avoid all that and focus on what you really care about.

After I got back to the fundamentals, I found myself getting more out of my interviews. I learned ideas to help me grow my business. I got marriage tips from people who were married much longer than me. And I laughed so hard you could hear me in every corner of our house.

Rediscovering these conversation techniques helped me enjoy interviewing so much that I started recording interviews with my wife and kids. It helped us spend focused time together, where I could hear their thoughts and experiences.

I'm curious to hear the interesting ways you end up using these ideas. Whether it's in a formal interview setting, like the one I've done for over a decade, or the more casual interviews I started doing with my family, I'd like to know how you use what you learned in this book. Email me about them: HeyAndrew@Mixergy.com.

Stop asking questions. Start leading high-impact interviews.

About the Author

Andrew Warner is an entrepreneur and host of the hit startup podcast, *Mixergy*, where he uncovers the secrets of the world's best founders. Over the course of 2,000+ episodes, Andrew has interviewed everyone from Barbara Corcoran, to Gary Vee, to the founders of Airbnb. After building two startups of his own—one successful and one failed—Andrew started *Mixergy* as a way to learn from other entrepreneurs. Today, Mixergy is a place where successful people teach ambitious upstarts through interviews, courses, master classes, and events.

When he's not interviewing, Andrew loves to spend time with his wife, Olivia, and their two children. Andrew is also an avid runner and has completed a marathon on every continent, including Antarctica.

Find him on Twitter at @AndrewWarner and @Mixergy.